CliffsNotes™

One Flew Over the Cuckoo's Nest

By Bruce Edward Walker

IN THIS BOOK

- ■ Learn about the Life and Background of the Author
- ■ Preview an Introduction to the Novel
- ■ Explore themes, style and language, and literary devices in the Critical Commentaries
- ■ Delve into in-depth Character Analyses
- ■ Reinforce what you learn with CliffsNotes Review
- ■ Find more *One Flew Over the Cuckoo's Nest* information in CliffsNotes Resource Center and online at www.cliffsnotes.com

Wiley Publishing, Inc.

About the Author

Bruce Walker is adjunct professor of literature and technical writing at the University of Detroit Mercy in Detroit, MI. He earned a B.A. in English from Michigan State University in 1985. He is a contributing editor to Gale Group's Literary Criticism Series, from 1985-2000. He was also an editor and a publisher of Detroit Athletic Club magazine, *DAC News*, from 1992-96. Bruce currently edits Ford Motor Company's Customer Relationship Management Web sites for J. Walter Thompson Advertising in Detroit, MI.

Publisher's Acknowledgments

Editorial

Project Editor: Colleen Williams Esterline

Acquisitions Editor: Greg Tubach

Copy Editor: Colleen Williams Esterline

Glossary Editors: The editors and staff of Webster's New World™ Dictionaries

Composition

Proofreader: York Production Services, Inc.

Indexer: York Production Services

Wiley Indianapolis Composition Services

CliffsNotes™ *One Flew Over the Cuckoo's Nest*

Published by:
Wiley Publishing, Inc.
111 River Street
Hoboken, NJ 07030
www.wiley.com

Table of Contents

LIFE AND BACKGROUND OF THE AUTHOR

Personal Background

Ken Kesey most often is characterized as the literary figure who bridged the Beat movement of the 1950s with the 1960s counterculture. This reputation springs from his literary themes of rebellion against societally imposed repression, which links him with the Beats, and his personal experiences as a volunteer in the U. S. government's experiments with psychotropic and hallucinogenic drugs. These latter experiences, coupled with his penchant for communal living and rock music, ensure his status as a preeminent spokesperson for the 1960s counterculture.

Kesey was born in La Junta, Colorado, in 1935. While he was still a child, he moved to Oregon with his family. After receiving his bachelor's degree from the University of Oregon in 1957, Kesey enrolled in the creative writing program at Stanford University. It was during his student tenure at Stanford that Kesey volunteered as an active participant in the testing of the psychotropic LSD and the hallucinogens mescaline (derived from the mescal or peyote cactus) and psilocybin (mushrooms) at the Veterans' Administration Hospital.

Kesey believed that the perception-altering LSD (in contrast to the actual hallucinogenic qualities of mescaline and psilocybin) was a tool useful for transcending rational consciousness and attaining a higher level of consciousness. Aside from Timothy Leary, whom Kesey met briefly during the Further Tour recounted in Tom Wolfe's *The Electric Kool-Aid Acid Test*, no person was a more vocal proponent for the use of LSD during the 1960s.

Kesey's interest in altered consciousness led him to accept a position in a mental hospital. While the job allowed him ample opportunity to write uninterrupted, it also introduced him to several individuals who would serve as models for characters in *One Flew Over the Cuckoo's Nest*. Kesey also ingested LSD (called "tripping") while interviewing the patients in order to gain insight into their altered perceptions of the world. He even convinced a friend to administer electroshock therapy to ensure an accurate depiction in his novel.

Cuckoo's Nest conveys Kesey's interest in altered consciousness, particularly in the voice of the narrator, Chief Bromden. The paranoid sections of the novel where Chief discusses his belief that the hospital where he stays is actually an emasculating factory for a larger Combine that represses individuality were largely written while Kesey was under the influence of mind-altering substances.

Following the publication of *One Flew Over the Cuckoo's Nest*, Kesey formed The Merry Pranksters, a group that included Neal Cassady, Jack Kerouac's friend and inspiration for the character Dean Moriarty in the Beat novel *On the Road*. The Merry Pranksters were best known for conducting Acid Tests, which featured live music performed by the nascent Grateful Dead, psychedelic light shows, and the ingesting copious amounts of LSD 25 (lysergic acid diethylamide), a synthetic psychotropic drug that distorts perceptions and often creates an intense and lengthy euphoric experience. The Merry Pranksters also traveled across the United States in an old school bus they named "Further."

The success of his novel enabled Kesey to purchase a farm outside La Honda, California. His and the Merry Pranksters' increasingly public experiments with LSD led to legal investigations into their activities. His continued taunting of U.S. drug enforcement policies led him to flee to Mexico to avoid prosecution and then return to face imprisonment.

Upon his release, he returned to his family's farm in Oregon, where he raised four children with his wife, whom he married in 1957.

Career Highlights

Besides *One Flew Over the Cuckoo's Nest*, Kesey went on to write *Sometimes a Great Notion* (published by Viking in 1964), *Kesey's Garage Sale* (published by Viking in 1973), *The Day After Superman Died* (published by Lord John Press in 1980), *Demon Box* (published by Viking in 1986), *The Further Inquiry* (published by Viking in 1990), *Little Tricker the Squirrel Meets Big Double the Bear* (published by Viking in 1990), *The Sea Lion* (published by Viking in 1991), *Sailor Song* (published by Viking in 1992), and *Last Round Up*, with Ken Babbs, (published by Viking in 1994).

Despite the publication of other works, including the novel *Sometimes a Great Notion*, which became the film *Never Give an Inch* with Paul Newman and Henry Fonda, Kesey never recaptured the success of his first novel. In the late 1990s, he gathered several surviving members of the Merry Pranksters and drove across the United States in a new version of the bus Further.

INTRODUCTION TO THE NOVEL

Introduction to the Novel

Kesey relates the story of the clash between the repressive and rebellious wills, respectively, of Nurse Ratched and Randle Patrick McMurphy from the viewpoint of a paranoid schizophrenic named Chief Bromden. With the exception of a fishing excursion led by McMurphy with an accompanying doctor and eleven patients, the entire novel is set in the psychiatric hospital where McMurphy may or may not be feigning insanity to escape the hard labor of a work farm. The patients are classified either as Acutes or Chronics; the former considered curable and whose stay at the hospital is voluntary; while the latter are failed attempts of the hospital's staff to force its conformity on patients through electroshock therapy and lobotomies. The Acutes have succumbed to incomplete lives wherein the arbitrary whims of an increasingly mechanized and feminized society has emasculated them and rendered them ineffectual.

McMurphy invigorates the Acutes and the Chronic Chief with his open, frank heterosexuality, anti-academic, and rebellious approach to life. This contrasts strongly with Nurse Ratched's attempts to control the men, inevitably leading to a series of comically rendered showdowns. The novel turns more serious, however, when the men begin to adopt McMurphy's attitudes, resulting in Nurse Ratched's escalation of her repressive tactics. Increasingly relying on New Testament portrayals of the Passion and crucifixion of Jesus Christ, Chief relates Ratched's victory over McMurphy when she has him lobotomized. Her victory is short-lived, however, as McMurphy's lessons to the men result in many of the Acutes leaving the hospital. Chief suffocates McMurphy and escapes from the hospital, in an ending that is both heroic and ambiguous.

Brief Synopsis

Chief Bromden, the son of a Native American father and a white mother, begins the novel by relating the real and imagined humiliations he suffers at the hands of the African-American hospital assistants. While their treatment of him is tolerated, despite the fact that he is physically much larger than they are, Chief expresses a greater fear of Big Nurse, Nurse Ratched. The Nurse is identified as a woman of great power and control, who is bitter because her ruthless, machine-like efficiency is thwarted by her naturally endowed large breasts. Despite her power, the paranoid-schizophrenic Chief believes her to be in service of the Combine, a large mechanized matrix that hums behind the walls and floors of the hospital, controlling everything from the environment to human behavior.

Randle Patrick McMurphy is introduced as a new patient on the ward. McMurphy immediately distinguishes himself from the other patients in the disregard he displays for all authority. He gambles, swears, makes off-color sexual remarks, and immediately sets himself in opposition to Nurse Ratched. McMurphy verbalizes his views that Ratched is a "ball-cutter." She controls the men by encouraging them to spy on each other and participate in group sessions where they verbally brutalize each other. At first they defend Ratched, but eventually agree with McMurphy's assessment. He attempts to assert his newfound leadership role among the patients by requesting permission to watch the World Series on the ward's television set. When this permission is denied, he turns the television on anyway. Because she controls power, Ratched shuts off the electricity to the television. McMurphy, however, gets the upper hand by insisting on watching a blank screen, an action imitated by the other patients.

In Part 2 of the novel, a lifeguard, who is involuntarily committed to the hospital like McMurphy, tells McMurphy that he must adhere to Ratched's rules or risk her extending his sentence indefinitely. He backs off from his rebellious behavior, but he has already sowed the seeds of rebellion in his fellow patients. When McMurphy fails to support the patient Cheswick in his assertions that he should have access to his cigarettes, the disillusioned man commits suicide by drowning himself in the pool where McMurphy first decided to "toe the line." Following this event, McMurphy is told that the other Acutes have committed themselves of their own volition, and that they can leave whenever they please. He returns to his rebellious behavior, smashing a window to get at the cigarettes, a symbolic action that alludes to Cheswick's lost battle with Ratched. Ratched, in turn, remains passive, waiting for McMurphy to make a mistake.

Part 3 of the novel relates McMurphy's successful attempt to take several of the patients on a fishing trip. Ratched tries to scare the meeker patients away from the trip by posting newspaper clippings of bad weather and boating accidents, but the men muster their courage and go anyway. Accompanying the men on the trip is Doctor Spivey, a morphine addict who is blackmailed by Ratched to acknowledge her authority, and Candy Starr, a young prostitute who proudly displays her physical feminine attributes. The trip galvanizes the group, and they return to the hospital to exhibit their newfound individuality.

Part 4 begins with Ratched's attempts to make the other patients suspicious of McMurphy's motives. She manipulates the conversation to make it appear that McMurphy acts only out of self-interest. This assertion appears valid to Chief, who allows McMurphy to use his strength to win a bet against the other patients. McMurphy, however, redeems himself in the eyes of the other men when he defends another patient from receiving an enema from a belligerent hospital aide. A fight ensues, and Chief assists McMurphy. The two win the fight but are sent to the Disturbed Ward. When McMurphy refuses to apologize, he and Chief are given electroshock therapy.

Chief returns to the ward before McMurphy, and discovers that he and McMurphy are now heroes to the other men. He reveals to the patients his ability to speak and tells the men about McMurphy. McMurphy's absence from the ward increases his legend among the men. When he eventually returns, McMurphy attempts to hide the mental strain he is enduring with a false show of bravado. While the other men have regained their sanity and sense of individuality, McMurphy begins to behave like a parody of his old self. The other patients realize that McMurphy is in a delicate state and plot his escape. He refuses, however, in order to honor a commitment he made to Billy Bibbit. Bibbit, a 31-year-old virgin, had made a date with the prostitute Candy Starr, and McMurphy vows to stay until Bibbit and Starr have sex.

Starr and another prostitute smuggle themselves onto the ward with liquor, which, combined with the marijuana provided by the African-American night watchman, Mr. Turkle, contribute to a night of debauchery. The patients make a mess of the ward and fall asleep after planning McMurphy's escape with Starr. Everyone sleeps late, and McMurphy remains in the hospital when Ratched arrives the following morning. The group remains defiantly united against Ratched until she discovers Bibbit sleeping with Starr. She tells Bibbit that his mother will learn of his indiscretion, forcing Bibbit to betray his fellow patients in general and McMurphy in particular. Bibbit slits his throat while waiting alone in Doctor Spivey's office, an action that Ratched blames on McMurphy's influence. McMurphy responds by attempting to strangle her. He fails, but rips open her uniform to expose her large breasts, revealing her sexuality, which weakens her authority over the patients.

McMurphy is removed to the Disturbed Ward, and many of the patients assert their prerogative to leave the hospital. When he is returned, the remaining patients doubt the lobotomized body is actually

McMurphy. When it is ascertained that it is indeed he, Chief suffocates him and escapes.

While Chief's escape is often interpreted as McMurphy's final victory over Ratched, some critics are less certain. For example, the novel's first five pages are related as occurring in the present and recount observations of the hospital ward, hinting that perhaps Chief has been recommitted and that the Combine eventually wins. Chief relates that a bluetick hound smells his own "fear burning down into him like steam." He writes, "It's gonna burn me just that way, finally telling about all this, about the hospital, and her, and the guys—and about McMurphy."

List of Characters

Randle Patrick McMurphy   A manual laborer, gambler, carnival barker, Korean War hero with a dishonorable discharge, and con man admitted to the ward from Pendelton Prison Farm, diagnosed as a psychotic. Really not insane, he transforms the ward by teaching the other inmates to question arbitrary and repressive authority. Eventually lobotomized after attacking Nurse Ratched, he is killed in his sleep by Chief Bromden.

Nurse Ratched   The "Big Nurse," and former Army nurse. She maintains order by exercising absolute authority over the hospital staff and its patients. McMurphy compares her techniques with the "brainwashing" used by the Communists during the Korean conflict.

Chief Bromden   A towering man of mixed Native American and white heritage. He is diagnosed as an incurable paranoid-schizophrenic, and pretends to be deaf and mute in order to protect himself from the forces of the Combine, which he believes is a mechanized society intent on usurping freedom and individuality. The Chief is gradually rehabilitated by McMurphy and emerges as the real protagonist of the book at the conclusion. He suffocates McMurphy after Nurse Ratched has him lobotomized and escapes from the hospital.

Dale Harding   A college-educated and effeminate man, who is psychologically "castrated" by his sexy wife and Nurse Ratched. Harding is an Acute patient, one who has voluntarily committed himself to the hospital.

Billy Bibbit   A 31-year-old man dominated by his mother to the extent that he is still unmarried and a virgin. Bibbit is also a voluntarily committed Acute, despite the fact that his wrists reveal a previous suicide attempt.

Max Taber   A rebellious patient whose presence on the ward preceded McMurphy's. He was released from the hospital after being made docile by electroshock therapy.

Scanlon   The last of McMurphy's followers left on the ward, he assists in the Chief's escape after McMurphy's death.

Cheswick   The first patient to adopt McMurphy's rebellious stance. After McMurphy begins to yield to authority, Cheswick drowns himself.

Martini   A delusional man, who, nonetheless, learns to laugh at himself and the world around him.

Sefelt and Frederickson   Both men are epileptics. Sefelt refuses to take his medicine because it causes his gums to rot and his teeth to fall out; Frederickson, on the other hand, takes double dosages.

Big George (Rub-a-Dub)   A Scandinavian former seaman with a morbid fear of dirt. He is captain of the boat on the fishing trip, and his fear of an enema causes McMurphy and Chief to defend him against the African-American hospital aides.

The Lifeguard   A former football player given to fits of violent behavior. Like McMurphy, his commitment is involuntary. He explains to McMurphy that they can only be released when Ratched signs their releases.

Tadem and Gregory   Two Acutes who join McMurphy on the fishing excursion.

Pete Bancini   A patient who, like McMurphy, avoided the controlling influence of the Combine, but suffers from brain damage.

Colonel Matterson   A wheelchair-bound patient who raves continually in disconnected metaphors.

Ellis and Ruckly   Two Acutes turned to Chronics after receiving too much electroshock. Ellis stands in a posture of a crucifixion against the ward walls.

Old Rawler   A noisy patient in Disturbed. He bleeds to death after castrating himself.

Old Blastic   A "vegetable" who dies in his sleep during Chief's hallucination of the Combine's mechanized butcher shop.

Doctor Spivey   A morphine addict, chosen by Nurse Ratched to work on her ward because she can exploit his weakness and vulnerability. He nevertheless begins to assert himself after continued exposure to McMurphy's behavior.

Nurse with a Birthmark   A perpetually frightened and attractive young nurse. She defends herself from perceived threats by McMurphy by protesting that she is a Catholic, indicating her sense of guilt and fear of sex.

Japanese Nurse   The one example of a woman in the novel who mediates the two extremes of "ball-cutter" and whore. She disagrees with Nurse Ratched's methods.

The "Black Boys" (Washington, Warren, and Geever)
Chosen by Nurse Ratched as orderlies because of their hostility and strength. They keep order on the ward mainly by threatening the patients and each other.

Mr. Turkle   An elderly African-American night watchman who smokes marijuana. McMurphy bribes him to help arrange the novel's final party.

Candy Starr   A prostitute from Portland with a "heart of gold." She is physically attractive and passive, and relieves Billy Bibbit of his virginity.

Sandy Gilfilliam   Candy's older and less-physically attractive friend; comes with her to the party on the ward.

Captain Block   Captain of the fishing boat stolen by the patients. His relationship with McMurphy is initially adversarial, but the two men wind up getting drunk together.

Character Map

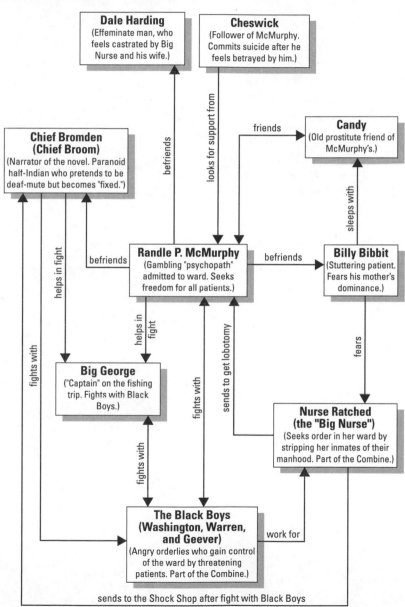

Dale Harding
(Effeminate man, who feels castrated by Big Nurse and his wife.)

Cheswick
(Follower of McMurphy. Commits suicide after he feels betrayed by him.)

Candy
(Old prostitute friend of McMurphy's.)

Chief Bromden (Chief Broom)
(Narrator of the novel. Paranoid half-Indian who pretends to be deaf-mute but becomes "fixed.")

friends

looks for support from

befriends

Randle P. McMurphy
(Gambling "psychopath" admitted to ward. Seeks freedom for all patients.)

befriends

befriends

helps in fight

sleeps with

Billy Bibbit
(Stuttering patient. Fears his mother's dominance.)

helps in fight

helps in fight

sends to get lobotomy

Big George
("Captain" on the fishing trip. Fights with Black Boys.)

fights with

fears

Nurse Ratched (the "Big Nurse")
(Seeks order in her ward by stripping her inmates of their manhood. Part of the Combine.)

fights with

fights with

The Black Boys (Washington, Warren, and Geever)
(Angry orderlies who gain control of the ward by threatening patients. Part of the Combine.)

work for

sends to the Shock Shop after fight with Black Boys

CRITICAL COMMENTARIES

Part 1
They're Out There

Summary

One of the "black boys" boasts to another that he can order Chief—who is "big enough to eat apples off my head"—to do his bidding, establishing Chief, the narrator of the story, as a large, passive, half-Indian. Chief can hear the men talking, which they do freely in his presence because they believe Chief is deaf. Not only does Chief hear the employees, he describes their conversation as the "hum of black machinery, humming hate and death and other hospital secrets."

Big Nurse Ratched enters the ward, and Chief describes her as carrying a wicker basket that contains the wheels and cogs she'll need to maintain the machinery of the Combine. He relates that her basket contains none of the feminine accoutrements one normally would imagine in a woman's purse.

Big Nurse catches the black boys' conversation, and Chief describes her resulting anger as a powerful force that inflates her size to as "big as a tractor," enabling him to "smell the machinery." She reverts to her original physical shape, however, when other patients enter the hall. She tells the employees to quit talking and go back to work, addressing them in an authoritative yet patronizing tone.

Chief describes Big Nurse's large breasts as a source of bitterness for her, because he believes she would have been a perfect machine without a woman's physical attributes to remind her that she is human. The rest of his description of Big Nurse refers to her less-than-human characteristics: a "smooth, calculated, and precision-made" face "like an expensive baby doll" and her "flesh-colored enamel" skin.

Big Nurse instructs the employees to shave Chief before breakfast, causing him to panic and hide in a closet. Chief informs the reader that he fears the Combine is more effective on its victims weakened by hunger. He remembers himself back to his youth on the Columbia River in Oregon, bird hunting with his father. Chief believes that the employees smell his fear the way that a bird dog smells a hunter's prey.

Discovered by the employees, Chief passively submits to his shave, because he believes that fighting would make his situation worse. He hallucinates that the Combine starts the fog machines while he screams louder and louder until Big Nurse comes to stifle his screaming by forcing her wicker basket into his mouth, using a mop handle.

Chief tells the reader that the story he is telling is about the horrors of the hospital, about Nurse Ratched, about an individual named McMurphy, and that it is difficult for him to relate to it. He swears his story is true "even if it didn't happen."

Commentary

The first section of this novel begins with the line, "They're out there," which establishes the paranoia of the novel's first-person narrator, Chief Bromden. Bromden, it becomes apparent later, is also schizophrenic. Bromden describes African-American employees wearing white suits, dirtying the hall by performing "sex acts" and mopping "up before I can catch them."

Theme

Chief's conviction that the ward is controlled by the Combine is evidence of his paranoia. He alludes to the Combine when he describes the employees' eyes "glittering out of the black faces like the hard glitter of radio tubes out of the back of an old radio," inferring that the employees are merely cogs in a much larger and much more foreboding machine.

Character Insight

Chief introduces Big Nurse, a woman he describes as carrying a large wicker basket in which she does not carry lipsticks, makeup, or other feminine beauty products. Chief believes that she uses the bag to carry replacement parts for the Combine. Chief depicts her as an individual who can increase her size at will, exhibiting her power over the other employees and the patients of the ward. He comments on Big Nurse's large breasts, which she attempts to conceal. He remarks that a "mistake was made somehow in manufacturing, putting those big, womanly breasts on what would of otherwise been a perfect work, and you can see how bitter she is about it."

Chief is so paranoid of the Combine that he fears that the electric shaver the orderlies use on him actually implants machinery in him. He hides in the closet, but the orderlies find him. He finds solace in his memories of bird hunting with his Indian father, and eventually succumbs to the fog that he believes is generated by the Combine.

Glossary

Here and in the following parts, different words and phrases, as well as allusions and historical references, are explained:

Combine a large mind- and environment-controlling mechanism concealed within the walls of the hospital.

The Dalles a geographic region located in Oregon, the setting of the novel.

fog the fog as used by Chief Bromden indicates his paranoid perception that the Combine emits a thick cloud when it needs to subdue and control the patients.

Part 1
When the Fog Clears

Summary

On this day, Chief is spared electroshock therapy in the Shock Shop. Instead, Big Nurse puts him in Seclusion where he suffers at the hands of the African-American orderlies. When he comes out, he sits in the day room and witnesses the admission of a new patient.

The new patient, Randle Patrick McMurphy, is loud, playful, and boisterous. Chief states that "he's no ordinary Admission," and furthermore exhibits no fear or passive behavior. McMurphy's voice reminds Chief of his father, who was a real Colombian Indian chief. McMurphy emits what Chief describes as "the first laugh I've heard in years," while admitting that all the other patients are afraid to laugh so they snicker into their hands instead.

McMurphy tells the patients that he was sent to the hospital because of scuffles he caused on a work farm, which caused the courts to label him a psychopath. He tells the patients that he isn't about to question the court's wisdom if it means getting out of performing manual labor on the work farm. He disagrees with his perception of the court's use of the term psychopath, because he feels the term denotes an individual "who fights too much and fucks too much." He immediately proceeds to make bets with his fellow patients.

Commentary

Character Insight

Chief describes McMurphy as "big," apparently oblivious to the fact that his own physical stature is substantially larger than McMurphy's. This is notable because Chief also refers to Nurse Ratched and his own mother as able to grow bigger in order to control their surroundings, while Chief feels powerless within his environment. The boisterousness of McMurphy reminds Chief of his father, who was also a big man in size and attitude.

Glossary

electroshock therapy   a form of shock therapy in which electric current is applied to the brain.

Shock Shop   a room on the hospital's Disturbed Ward where electroshock therapy is administered.

Part 1
The New Man

Summary

Chief describes the relationships of the men on the ward. He relates that the Big Nurse encourages them to divulge information on other patients by writing down into her log book what they overheard in conversation. Big Nurse rewards the individual who made the entry by allowing him to sleep later than the other patients, and uses this information in the group therapy sessions to turn the patients against one another.

Chief tells of the division between the Acutes and the Chronics on the ward. The Chronics are those that he describes as "the culls of the Combine's product." Some Chronics, he says, began their stay at the hospital as Acutes, but due to staff errors, became Chronics. Big Nurse threatens the Acutes exhibiting undesirable behavior that they may end up as Chronics, a foreshadowing of events that will eventually play out in the novel. Chief writes that the ward proudly exhibits a sign congratulating it for "GETTING ALONG WITH THE SMALLEST NUMBER OF PERSONNEL," which he believes is due to the passive cooperation of the Acute patients. The sign is a line of demarcation between the Acutes and the Chronics, placed there as an implicit warning to keep in line by Big Nurse.

Chief equates the patient's fear of female authority to schoolboys' fear of being caught acting naughty by their teacher. McMurphy, oblivious to their fear, challenges the Acutes to identify the "bull goose loony," which would be the "craziest" patient. He dismisses Billy Bibbit, a stuttering, 31-year-old man, and is introduced to Dale Harding, a college-educated, effeminate man. Chief relates enough information about Harding to indicate that he has been figuratively emasculated by his large-breasted wife and an education that has divorced his intellect from his masculinity.

Their curiosity raised, the patients ask McMurphy about his background. He tells them that he served in the Army, was a logger, learned to play poker, and is dedicated to staying single and gambling. He says he never had trouble with the law when he got into fights as a logger or soldier, but was persecuted for fighting when he became a gambler. He tells the other men that he is incarcerated for assault and battery.

McMurphy introduces himself to all the men on the ward and comes to Chief Bromden. Billy Bibbit explains that Chief is deaf, and that Bibbit would kill himself if he became deaf, a foreshadowing of his death.

Commentary

In this portion of the novel, Kesey seems to indicate that the methods of therapy used by Nurse Ratched are intended more to control the patients rather than cure them (for example, the destructive spying that she encourages between the Acutes exemplified by the log book). In addition, the orderlies emotionally torture the Chronics, as typified by the dwarf black orderly who "gets a rise out of him [Ruckly] from time to time by leaning close and asking, 'Say, Ruckly, what you figure your little wife is doing in town tonight?'"

Nurse Ratched keeps the Acutes and the Chronics on the same ward, apparently to frighten the Acutes with the possibility that they may end up as Chronics if they don't yield to her authority. Chief writes, "The Big Nurse recognizes this fear and knows how to put it to use; she's point out to an Acute, whenever he goes into a sulk, that you boys be good boys and cooperate with staff policy which is engineered for your *cure*, or you'll end up over on *that* side."

Chief introduces two of the Chronics, Ellis and Ruckly, both of whom he refers to as "culls of the Combine," and products of the "filthy brain-murdering room that the black boys call the 'Shock Shop.'" Speaking specifically about Ruckly, Chief believes that, although Nurse Ratched considers Ruckly one of her failures, perhaps he's "better off as a failure," rather than as a successful example of the Combine's machinations.

Glossary

chronic   lasting a long time or recurring often.

bull goose loony   an oxymoron. A bull indicates masculine qualities while a goose indicates feminine. A loony, of course, is someone not entirely in control of their mental faculties and perhaps unable to discern whether they are a bull or a goose.

Patient's Council   a group of Acutes appointed by other patients and Nurse Ratched, ostensibly, to vote on matters of interest to the other patients. Because none of the council members wants to upset Nurse Ratched, the group is essentially powerless.

voting for Eisenhower   Dwight Eisenhower was a World War II general and president of the United States during the latter half of the 1950s, a period perceived by many to be marked by conservatism and conformity. Therefore, one who votes for Eisenhower is a conformist.

Part 1

In the Glass Station

Summary

Chief overhears Big Nurse explain to Nurse Flinn, a young nurse, that McMurphy is a manipulator who had himself put in the hospital to escape work detail. Big Nurse explains that McMurphy reminds her of another patient, Mr. Taber. Maxwell Taber, Chief tells the reader later, was an Acute that Big Nurse had lobotomized and dismissed from the hospital.

Chief describes Big Nurse as a mechanical robot, manipulated by fine wires visible only to him that connect her to the Combine. She has been able to manipulate doctors into either conforming to her will or transferring elsewhere. He depicts the orderlies as handpicked by Big Nurse for their ability to hate and the easiness by which she can sterilize them into their pressed white uniforms.

Resident doctors make their rounds at 9 a.m. to have superficial discussions with the Acutes. The residents' presence annoys and worries Big Nurse because she can't control them. When they leave, Chief notices that the Combine's machinery runs smoothly again until the Public Relations man conducts a tour of the ward.

The humming of the Combine's machinery reminds Chief of when he played football in high school and the places the coach made the team visit. One of these places was a cotton mill in California where Chief met a young African-American girl who begged him to take her away.

Chief imagines Taber being dismissed from the hospital as a respected member of society, which would vindicate Big Nurse's methods. He foreshadows upcoming events when he says that, "Everybody's happy with a Dismissal," and begins talking about the methods to bring an Admission into the hospital's routine.

Commentary

Chief relates that Nurse Ratched runs the ward like a machine, and "gets real put out" if the machine isn't running smoothly. He believes that she also spends some of her time making adjustments to the machinery of the world outside the hospital as well. Through time, she has hired a staff that she uses as tools to regulate the Combine's machinery. Staff members that don't "fit" are discarded and replaced. The staff that remains, Chief tells the reader, is comprised of individuals who are on Nurse Ratched's "frequency."

Chief describes the hospital as an automotive mechanic's garage, where the employees require an alcoholic bracer before applying their trade. He imagines a staff member confessing, "It's getting I can't install the simplest frigging component but what I need a bracer. Well, what the hell, it's better'n garage work...." Later, Chief recounts that the hospital is nothing more than a garage for fixing the mistakes made by such societal elements as school and church. He believes that the hospital installs Delayed Reaction Elements in the patients who are cured, who, in turn, leave the hospital to install the same in their family members.

When the residents make their rounds of the ward, Chief says the machinery behind the walls of the hospital quiets until they leave again. During their visit, however, Chief relates that Nurse Ratched is suspicious of the young men with crew cuts. By 10:40 a.m. the machinery hums like a cotton mill.

Glossary

lobotomy   a surgical operation in which a lobe of the brain, especially the frontal lobe of the cerebrum, is cut into or across as a treatment for psychosis.

electroencephalograph   an instrument for making electroencephalograms, graphic tracings of minute voltage changes resulting from bioelectric activity in the brain.

pinochle   any of a family of card games, usually for three or four persons and typically played with a 48-card deck made up of two of every card above the eight, including the ace.

Part 1
Before Noontime

Summary

At 1 p.m., the Acutes assemble for their daily meeting with Big Nurse and Doctor Spivey. Big Nurse opens the session by reading notes that other patients have submitted on Dale Harding. Big Nurse asks if any member of the group would like to touch upon the matter further. McMurphy uses the opportunity to make an off-color remark about touching the breasts of Harding's wife, a statement that catches Big Nurse off guard and flusters her.

To cover her frustration, Big Nurse reads McMurphy's file. He received a Distinguished Service Cross in Korea for leading an escape from a prison camp, but was dishonorably discharged for fighting and insubordination. He also was once charged with the statutory rape of a 15-year-old girl. McMurphy says that the girl's insatiable sexual appetite made him take "to sewing my pants shut," and that he was forced to leave town because the girl would have "burnt me to a frazzle by the time she reached legal sixteen."

In his discussion with Doctor Spivey, McMurphy makes a veiled threat to Big Nurse and repeats that the work farm doctor has diagnosed him as a potential psychotic. Doctor Spivey responds that the doctor also suggests that McMurphy could be feigning mental instability to get out of work detail.

McMurphy's joking and Doctor Spivey's obvious enjoyment of his behavior cause Big Nurse to place control of the meeting back into the hands of Doctor Spivey.

McMurphy approaches Harding to discuss the meeting, calling it a "pecking party." Harding defends Big Nurse, but McMurphy refers to her as "a bitch and a buzzard and a ball-cutter." Harding tries to refute McMurphy but ends up convincing himself that McMurphy is correct.

Commentary

During the meeting, Ratched exerts control over the patients by her autocratic demeanor. Because Harding is the group's most intelligent and educated member, she begins the meeting by reminding him that his wife's physical attractiveness makes him feel insecure. The meeting concludes with Chief's observation that McMurphy is learning quickly about the group in order to make a gambler's move at a later time.

McMurphy tells Harding that Big Nurse set up Harding to take the pecks of his fellow patients whom McMurphy calls "bastards." Harding argues that the session was for his benefit, to which McMurphy responds that Big Nurse wasn't pecking at his eyes, she was pecking lower, referring to his masculinity. McMurphy tells Harding that the session weakened Harding because everyone attacked him where it hurt worse, in his "vitals," which is where people who want to make someone weak rather than make themselves stronger prefer to strike.

He tells McMurphy that the patients are the victims of a matriarchy established by a female supervisor who condones Big Nurse's methods. Doctor Spivey is ineffectual because, as Harding says, Big Nurse can report him for writing large requisitions for Demerol. This last fact can be interpreted that Doctor Spivey is addicted to the morphine that is Demerol's active pain-killing ingredient. Harding calls the patients and Doctor Spivey rabbits and Nurse Ratched a wolf. Worse, Harding says that they are rabbits without sexual potency. The conversation leads to a bet that McMurphy can get Nurse Ratched's goat within a week. Harding allows McMurphy to hold the bets, because, as he says to McMurphy, "You won't be going any place for a while."

Glossary

matriarchy   government, rule, or domination by women.

Part 1
One Christmas

Summary

Chief tells of a visitor to the ward six years before, who was dressed as Santa Claus with a natural beard. He is "fixed" and sent out into the world clean shaven and underweight.

McMurphy complains that the ward radio is playing too loud and asks Nurse Ratched to turn down the volume, a request that she refuses due to the her belief that the ward's patients who are hearing impaired will not be able to enjoy the music.

McMurphy discovers Chief isn't deaf when he tells him an orderly is coming to tie him into bed and Chief responds immediately.

Commentary

Character Insight

The story of Santa Claus indicates that the Combine is able to change even the most innocuous and innocent individual from a happy, full-bodied and bearded individual into a conformist. This indicates why Chief pretends to be deaf and mute, because he believes the Combine won't take from him what it doesn't know he possesses, and if he is able to keep his secret, the Combine can't control him completely. McMurphy discovers Chief's secret accidentally, but his discovery allows both McMurphy and the reader to see that Chief is curable, and that his ability to overcome his fear of speaking is crucial to his recovery.

Part 1
First Time for a Long, Long Time

Summary

Chief doesn't take his sleeping pill and hallucinates about the Combine and its horrors through the night until he's awakened by Turkle, an elderly African American who works the night shift. One of the subjects of Chief's hallucination is the patient Blastic, who coincidentally dies during the night.

Commentary

Literary
Device

Chief's hallucination takes him on a nightmarish trip to what he believes lies beneath the hospital floor. He envisions the machinery of the Combine pumping fog and eviscerating Blastic. He imagines the hospital's Public Relations man conducting a tour for school teachers and college co-eds. The Public Relations man collects trophies—body parts of the patients—and hangs them from his shirt. By this hallucination, the reader may surmise that Kesey perceives the world outside the hospital as a mechanized, conformist environment that is prepared to destroy in the most vile and despicable fashion those who dare to challenge it.

Part 1
Come Morning

Summary

The next morning, McMurphy shocks the ward by singing. He asks an aide for toothpaste, but is told that ward policy won't allow the toothpaste to be unlocked because patients might use it at their own discretion. McMurphy baits the aide into a philosophical argument that points out the absurd and arbitrary nature of the ward policy, and resorts to using soap powder to brush his teeth. This also reminds Chief of how his father used to frustrate government agents by using the same rhetorical techniques.

McMurphy is confronted by Big Nurse as he exits the latrine. He greets her as "Miss Rat-shed," wearing what appears to be nothing more than a towel. He insists that someone has stolen his clothes during the night. Nurse Ratched realizes that McMurphy hasn't been issued his convalescent greens and chastises the aides, particularly one named Washington, for not doing their jobs, while McMurphy whistles "Sweet Georgia Brown." McMurphy winks at the nurse and removes the towel, revealing his whale-print undershorts to her. The shorts, he told Chief the night before, were a gift from a co-ed literature major. She gave him the shorts because she regarded McMurphy as "a symbol." The removal of the towel shocks Nurse Ratched, and she takes a while longer than usual to recover.

Commentary

Style &
Language

McMurphy's mispronunciation of Nurse Ratched's name indicates to the reader that her name indicates aspects of her personality. Rat-shed, obviously, has negative connotations, but the name is also similar sounding to "ratchet" and "wretched."

Chief writes that McMurphy's nonconformist behavior reminds him of his Indian father. Both men, he writes, liked to "get the goat" of other men by employing outlandish behavior and nonsequitors to baffle their more rigid opponents.

Glossary

croon   to sing or hum in a low, gentle tone; to sing (popular songs) in a soft, sentimental manner.

Part 1
All Through Breakfast

Summary

At breakfast, McMurphy teases Billy Bibbit, calling him Billy Club Bibbit with a legendary 14-inch penis. He invents a story about Bibbit picking up two prostitutes—"twitches"—and shocking one of them with the prodigious size of his member. The tale embarrasses Bibbit, but also gives him a sense of pride at being the hero of such an outlandish adventure. McMurphy further entertains the Acutes during breakfast by taking bets that he can shoot butter patties at the mess hall clock.

Later in the morning, McMurphy asks Nurse Ratched if she can turn down the music in the ward. Ratched tells him that he's being selfish, and that the music's volume is adjusted for the ward's hard of hearing. McMurphy suggests that he and the Acutes be allowed to play cards in another room where the music can't be heard. She rebuffs his idea, but McMurphy discusses it with Doctor Spivey, who believes the idea has merit. He also suggests that the ward host a carnival, something Chief remembers Max Taber suggested in the past. The additional room for card playing is approved against Ratched's wishes. Chief relates that McMurphy has won a battle, but is certain he'll lose the war.

Commentary

Character
Insight

McMurphy's behavior is becoming contagious among his fellow patients, invigorating them and endearing him to them. He is able to discern the perceived weaknesses of his new friends and turn them into their strengths. For example, he recasts Billy Bibbit as a swaggering ladies' man, and Chief as a large, self-confident individual.

Chief also details the escalating battle of wills between McMurphy and Nurse Ratched. At first flustered by McMurphy and his newfound popularity with the Acutes, Ratched is beginning to regain her controlled composure. This indicates to Chief that she's waiting for McMurphy to make a mistake before she makes her next move.

Glossary

twitch(es) a slang expression for a woman of easy virtue; a prostitute.

Part 1
There's a Monopoly Game

Summary

McMurphy joins the patients in an unorganized game of Monopoly. McMurphy, of course, ends up owning all the properties and winning all of the other players' money.

Commentary

At this point of the novel, McMurphy owns a monopoly on individuality. His nonconformity allows him to "win" where the other patients "lose."

Part 1
There's Long Spells

Summary

McMurphy's next battle with Ratched concerns allowing the patients to watch the World Series. Because the games are telecast during the ward's non-regulation television viewing time, McMurphy requests that the time be altered. Ratched refuses at first, then allows a vote of the patients. The other Acutes are afraid to vote against Nurse Ratched's wishes, however. After losing the vote, McMurphy says he and Charles Cheswick are going to break out a window in order to go to town to visit a bar and watch the game.

The patients bet that McMurphy can't lift a large control panel to throw through the window. He loses the bet, but tells the other patients that at least he tried.

Commentary

McMurphy's bet with the patients is one he knows he's sure to lose, but by losing he will win their trust that he's not always motivated by self-interest. By taking the bet, he displays to the patients that it is better to try something and fail rather than not try at all.

Part 1
A Visiting Doctor

Summary

This brief portion features Chief's recounting of an old doctor who visits the hospital. The doctor observes Chief and, by implication, the other patients as bugs. Chief imagines himself escaping the hospital through a picture hung in the ward, depicting a fly fisherman in a rustic scene. He remembers the hospital where he stayed before being transferred to Nurse Ratched's care, and recalls that it was much worse than what he is currently experiencing. He witnesses the visiting doctor shivering, and wonders if he feels the cold from the snow-capped peaks of the mountains in the picture.

Commentary

Character Insight

Chief is not ready to declare himself recovered. He rationalizes that the condition of his current care is better than what he has experienced in the past, so therefore it must be the best of all conceivable worlds. This despite the fact that he is familiar with the scene in the photograph that he imagines escaping into.

Part 1
It's Getting Hard

Summary

This one-paragraph portion reveals Chief's relapse into paranoia. He imagines the fog increasing, forcing him to crawl on the floor to find the gum he hides beneath his bed. He writes that McMurphy doesn't understand that the patients only want to be safe and not let him drag them out of the fog.

Commentary

Literary Device

Chief speaks for himself and the other patients. He perceives that a showdown will soon occur between Nurse Ratched and McMurphy, and fears that the fallout from the battle will negatively impact the other patients. In this respect, he believes that the devil he knows is better than the devil he doesn't know.

Part 1
There's a Shipment of Frozen Parts

Summary

Another of Chief's hallucinations, this one reveals Chief's perception that human body parts are being delivered to the hospital. Chief also writes that a patient on the Disturbed Ward performed a castration on himself and subsequently dies. Chief remarks that he considers this man's suicide an act of impatience, as everyone dies eventually.

Commentary

Literary
Device

Chief's opinion that life in the hospital is simply a waiting room for his eventual death reveals that he, and more than likely the other patients, have not yet learned how to live.

Part 1
I Know How They Work It

Summary

The conclusion of Part 1 begins with a stream of consciousness passage by Chief Bromden that details the extent of his paranoia and some of his mental condition's causes. He first experiences the fog while serving in the military during World War II. He believes the fog machine used on the ward is Army Surplus. He senses that the Combine is increasing the output of the fog machine until it can find a way to control McMurphy.

At a group meeting, McMurphy tells Nurse Ratched that he'd like another vote to change the television viewing schedule. Nurse Ratched realizes that McMurphy will never win a vote because she counts the votes of the Chronics as well as the Acutes, and the Chronics are not cognizant enough to understand what they're voting for. Ratched ends the meeting before a final vote is tallied; a tally that favors McMurphy and the Acutes. While the other patients are disillusioned, McMurphy denies Ratched her victory by placing himself in front of the television. When she shuts off the power, he and the other Acutes stay fixed to the television while Ratched yells at them to resume their duties. McMurphy has won another battle.

Commentary

McMurphy's actions serve to invigorate the Acutes who previously had resigned themselves to the leading of passive emasculated lives. While McMurphy's actions were initially perceived by Nurse Ratched and the patients alike as simply rebellious troublemaking, the patients begin to see it as a source of liberation. Realizing this, the reader may infer that Nurse Ratched will react in an opposite fashion than the patients.

Glossary

paranoid   characterized by extreme suspiciousness, grandiose delusions, or delusions of persecution.

paranoid schizophrenia   a chronic form of schizophrenia characterized by hallucinations, grandiose delusions, delusions of persecution, and so on.

maudlin   foolishly and tearfully or weakly sentimental.

Part 2
Just at the Edge of My Vision

Summary

The second section of this novel begins with the patients still watching the blank television screen. All except McMurphy, however, are completely aware of Ratched's anger. Even the orderlies and aides watch Ratched to see how she will react to the insubordinate behavior. Chief remarks that "there's no more fog anyplace," indicating that he believes McMurphy's rebellious behavior has removed it.

Chief is led to the staff room, where Nurse Ratched will conduct a staff meeting. Chief tells the reader that cleaning the staff room is a frightening chore because the staff emits poisonous and acidic gases and fluids. At times, Chief says, the staff is able to make a patient materialize on the table, "vulnerable to any fiendish notion they took."

The staff room is tense, and Nurse Ratched reacts suspiciously to Chief's presence. In a humorously and satirically written discussion, the staff debates what they should do with the impertinent McMurphy. The staff, described by Chief as "boys," attempts to anticipate Ratched's wishes by recommending that he be sent to the Disturbed Ward. Ratched disagrees, telling the staff that McMurphy is her responsibility and that she isn't prepared to admit failure this soon. She declares that McMurphy resembles Charles Cheswick, a man she says backs down when challenged. She reminds the staff that the length of McMurphy's stay at the hospital is entirely dependent on the determination of the staff based upon his ability to conform.

Commentary

Chief describes the hospital before the staff meeting that Nurse Ratched calls. Prior to the meeting, he states: "I notice all the machinery in the wall is quiet, like it's waiting for her to move," as if Nurse Ratched controls all of the hospital's apparatus, including all the staff members. This is contrasted with Chief's observation that "there's no more fog any place" when he enters the hallway, which gives the impression that McMurphy's actions have stymied Nurse Ratched and the Combine.

In depicting the meeting, Kesey satirizes the psychology profession as a group of individuals eager to ascribe Latinate labels to McMurphy's behavior.

Style & Language

Chief also uses temperature images to describe Nurse Ratched. Alternately frigid cold and scorching hot depending on her moods, both excessive temperatures indicate that she is somehow more machine than human. Prior to the meeting he recognizes, "It's a little cold where the nurse just went past, and the white tubes in the ceiling circulate frozen like rods of glowing ice, like frosted refrigerator coils rigged up to glow white." During the meeting, however, when she has the attention of the meeting members, she devises her plan to break McMurphy's spirit. When she decides what course of action she is going to pursue, she takes her first sip of coffee. Chief notices that "the cup comes away from her mouth with that red-orange color on it.... That color on the rim of the cup must be from heat, touch of her lips set it smoldering."

Part 2

The Way the Big Nurse Acted

Summary

McMurphy continues to bedraggle Ratched and her staff, while entertaining the patients with stories of his experiences. Chief observes McMurphy as an "enormous thing," and feels small by comparison, even though Chief is 6'7" tall. He says that McMurphy likes to paint pictures and writes with a perfect hand. He recognizes McMurphy as a man in control of his own life.

During the night, Chief awakens and notices that all the fog is cleared. He unties himself and looks out the window, where he observes a dog sniffing gopher holes by the light of the moon. The mongrel rolls playfully in the grass, shaking moisture off it "like silver scales."

A flock of geese flies in front of the moon, changing their V formation temporarily into "a black cross opening and closing." The dog follows the trail of the geese toward a road and an oncoming car. Chief watches as the dog and the car make "for the same spot of pavement," but doesn't find out what happens because a nurse and an aide put him back to bed.

Commentary

Character Insight

Chief's admiration of McMurphy increases, and he notices that the other patients also are gaining respect for him. He marvels that the Combine has gotten to him and the other patients, but not to McMurphy. He recognizes that McMurphy isn't extraordinary, but simply who he is, which he observes is enough to foil Nurse Ratched. Chief contrasts his impressions of McMurphy with his own reflection in the mirror. He sees a reflection that he refuses to believe is his. The reflection is a large man with chiseled features, but Chief admits that "It wasn't even me when I was trying to be that face.... It don't seem like I've ever been me. How can McMurphy be what he is?"

Literary Device

When Chief observes the dog from the hospital window, the reader is inclined to believe the dog symbolizes McMurphy. The dog casts a long shadow and lolls on the grass in the moonlight. He recounts that the dog runs toward the road as he hears "a car speed up out of a turn. The headlights loomed over the rise and peered ahead down the highway. I watched the dog and the car making for the same spot of pavement." The reader can infer that Chief is foreshadowing the fate of McMurphy as a force of nature destined to fail against the forces of mechanization.

Part 2
In the Group Meetings

Summary

Chief recounts that the group meetings have become gripe sessions now that the patients have been empowered by McMurphy's rebelliousness. They challenge Ratched's easy and often arbitrary rationales. Although she doesn't challenge McMurphy, he suspects that "she acts like she still holds all the cards up that white sleeve of hers."

McMurphy's suspicions are confirmed when he and the other patients are taken to the hospital pool. The lifeguard, who is sentenced like McMurphy, tells him that their respective stays are indefinite. Unlike the prison, when an inmate knows when he will be released, a patient in a mental institution is at the mercy of his keepers.

This revelation marks a change in McMurphy's behavior. He begins to become an exemplary patient, cleaning the latrine thoroughly and keeping his wisecracks to a minimum. His behavior confuses the other patients, and they speculate that he may be plotting a new, more blatant campaign against Ratched or else he's conforming by deciding to "toe the line." Cheswick looks to McMurphy to support him in an argument with Ratched, but McMurphy ignores him. Cheswick, "punctured," is taken to the Disturbed Ward, and Chief can again see the refrigerated light generated by the Combine. Chief, knowing the truth, states that McMurphy is being cagey, much like Chief's father was with the government agents who took his tribe's land.

When Cheswick returns to the ward, he visits the pool with the other patients. He tells McMurphy he understands why McMurphy is conforming. He then proceeds to deliberately drown himself by attaching himself to an underwater grate.

Commentary

Character Insight

After helping the patients recognize that they have been victimized by Ratched's autocratic methods, McMurphy withdraws in order to gain her favor to ensure an early release. The patients, especially Bibbit and Cheswick, perceive this as a sellout. Cheswick's feeling of betrayal is perhaps more telling, because Chief recalls that, during his tantrum at the group meeting, "He never had looked big; he was short and too fat and had a bald spot...but standing there by himself in the center of the day room like that he looked tiny." Whereas each of the patients eventually "grows" bigger when they empower themselves through their association with McMurphy, Cheswick doesn't spend enough time with the rebellious McMurphy in order to grow larger. Instead he commits suicide.

Glossary

latrine   a toilet, privy, etc. for the use of a large number of people.

gurney   a stretcher or cot on wheels, used in hospitals to move patients.

Part 2
Up Ahead of Me

Summary

In the lunch room, the patient Sefelt has an epileptic seizure because he has refused to take his medication. The medication, Dilantin, prevents seizures, but he saves it to give to Frederickson, another epileptic patient. Dilantin is an anticonvulsant, Frederickson tells McMurphy, as an orderly sweeps up two teeth that have fallen from Sefelt's mouth, that rots the gums of those who take it.

Commentary

Nurse Ratched seizes the opportunity of Sefelt's seizure to warn the patients that ignoring her medical advice can result in grave physical consequences. The veiled threat she gives is that if each and every patient doesn't toe the line and follow her orders, then they all run the risk of having something negative happen to them.

Glossary

convulsion   a violent, involuntary contraction or spasm of the muscles.

Part 2
Whatever It Was

Summary

Chief observes that the Combine is running near optimum efficiency again, and that Big Nurse is running the controls.

Commentary

McMurphy's withdrawal into conformity has reinvigorated the Combine. The sterile, white hands of Nurse Ratched once again operate the controls of the Combine.

Part 2

They Take Me with the Acutes Sometimes

Summary

Chief accompanies the Acutes to the library, where Harding is visited by his wife. Harding introduces her to McMurphy. She tells McMurphy to call her by her first name, Vera, rather than Mrs. Harding. She insults Harding's laugh as a "mousy little squeak," which aggravates Harding. When she asks for a cigarette, Harding has none, prompting her to state in an emasculating fashion, "Oh Dale, you never do have enough, do you?" Harding challenges the statement, but allows his challenge to dwindle to nothing more than a grammatical correction.

McMurphy reservedly gives Vera a cigarette, saying he only has a supply because he bums them from the other patients. As he lights her cigarette, Vera leans before him to provide a clear view down her blouse. She insults Harding's friends, who stop by their house looking for him. She remarks on the friends' "limp little wrists that flip so nice," and she implies that she's being unfaithful with at least one of his friends.

When she leaves, McMurphy tells Harding that he doesn't feel sorry for him. He says that he has his own worries and doesn't have time to think about the troubles of the other patients. He later apologizes to Harding, but refuses to play along with the patient Martini who pretends to see men strapped to the wall. McMurphy tells Martini that he doesn't care for his "sort of kidding," and mis-shuffles a deck of cards that explodes "between his two trembling hands."

Commentary

Theme

In this section, Chief observes that Harding's wife is an emasculating, "ball-cutting," flirt. Her actions imply that she is unfaithful because Harding is a weak lover and she has no use for his education. Kesey depicts Harding as an effeminate man whose education contributed to his emasculated state. The introduction of Mrs. Harding, however, evokes a sympathetic response toward Harding from the reader. Even though he denies it, McMurphy sympathizes as well, as evidenced by the pent-up aggression he displays after she leaves. Controlling his thoughts and angry impressions concerning Mrs. Harding causes him to lose control of the playing cards.

Part 2
I Remember It Was Friday Again

Summary

Harding explains the technology and history behind electroshock therapy, which began when psychiatrists observed the calm cattle experienced following a blow to the head with a sledgehammer. The resulting convulsions in some of the cattle resembled epileptic seizures. Inspired, they used electricity to induce seizures to calm upset patients. Harding tells McMurphy that he shouldn't worry about electroshock because, like lobotomies, the procedure is "out of vogue." But he also informs McMurphy that Nurse Ratched has the authority to order both procedures. Harding calls lobotomies a "frontal-lobe castration," adding that if Nurse Ratched "can't cut below the belt she'll do it above the eyes."

The patients discuss if Ratched is the source of the hospital's problems, and McMurphy pronounces his opinion that she is only one symptom of something larger and more malevolent. This pronouncement confirms Chief's belief in the Combine. McMurphy tells the Acutes that he's disappointed that they didn't tell him that rebelling against Nurse Ratched would make his life worse in the long run. They admit to him that they are voluntary inmates at the hospital and can leave whenever they want. They tell McMurphy that they are not as strong as he, which is why they prefer to stay committed.

Commentary

The descriptions of lobotomies and electroshock therapy are methods the Combine uses to control and change nonconformists. Once they are made to conform to society's standards, the patients are allowed to reenter society.

The Acutes' admission that they are voluntarily committed to the hospital comes after McMurphy admits he has been exhibiting good behavior in order to receive an early release. When he challenges the Acutes to actually attempt living their lives outside the hospital, Bibbit

Literary Device

emotionally tells him that none of them are as big and tough as McMurphy. McMurphy puts his hat back on, much like Gary Cooper before the final gun battle in the film *High Noon*.

Part 2
Crossing the Grounds

Summary

At the next group meeting, Ratched, feeling she now has the upper hand, tells the group that they will be punished for their rebellious behavior from three weeks ago. Telling them that the punishment is for their own good, she has decided to deny the use of the tub room for card playing. Thinking this is her final victory, Ratched is surprised when McMurphy rises from his chair. Chief writes that McMurphy regains his loggerman's stature as he approaches her. He stops before reaching her, however, and forces his hand through the glass of the nurses' station to retrieve his cigarettes, telling Ratched that the glass was so clean, he didn't know it was there. His return to true form stops the ringing in Chief's ears.

Commentary

Character Insight

The ringing in Chief's ears is a transmission from the Combine to the components installed in Chief's brain. When the ringing stops, it means that the Combine is flummoxed by something, which, in this instance, is McMurphy's return to nonconforming behavior.

Literary Device

Hooking his thumbs in the belt loops of his pants, McMurphy again adopts the stature of the Hollywood Western movie hero, swaggering toward the glass of the nurses' station. He refers to Nurse Ratched as "Ma'am" as Jimmy Stewart referred to Marlene Dietrich in the film *Destry Rides Again*. The reader is led to believe that a showdown of epic proportions is about to begin.

Glossary

Faulknerian   a reference to American writer and Nobel Laureate William Faulkner, known for his fiction that depicts human frailties.

Brain Burning   a reference to the effects of electroshock and a parody of the title of one of William Faulkner's more famous short stories, "Barn Burning."

punitive   inflicting, concerned with, or directed toward punishment.

leucotomy   lobotomy.

Part 3
After That

Summary

The third section of this novel begins with Chief recognizing that McMurphy's behavior also has infected Doctor Spivey. Spivey stands up to Ratched when she questions the wisdom of allowing the patients to play basketball on the ward.

The relationship between Ratched and McMurphy has become marked by a strained politeness until Ratched denies McMurphy an Accompanied Pass with a woman named Candy Starr. In response, McMurphy puts his hand through the glass of the nurses' station again, pretending it was an accident.

McMurphy coaches a game pitting the patients against the African-American aides that soon turns unruly. McMurphy bloodies the nose of the aide named Washington, which will impact future events in the novel.

The patients' behavior is changed because of McMurphy's influence. Harding flirts with the student nurses, Billy Bibbit stops writing about other patients in Ratched's log book, and Scanlon throws the basket-ball through the recently replaced glass in the nurses' station.

McMurphy applies for a pass for a fishing excursion that will include eight or nine patients, writing that he'll be accompanied by "two sweet old aunts." The pass is granted, but Ratched attempts to frighten the patients who will accompany him with a newspaper clipping about how rough the sea will be. She posts this clipping on a bulletin board, adding similar clippings of boating accidents as the excursion draws nearer.

Ratched's tactic frightens the Acutes, but Chief desires to go. He is concerned, however, that if he signs on, it will indicate to everyone that he has heard everything. He tells the reader, "I had to keep on acting deaf if I wanted to hear at all." He remembers that the first time his presence wasn't felt was when he was ten years old. At that time, three white people visited the Chief's family and behaved as if Chief wasn't present. They disparaged the living conditions of Chief's family and discussed how they should approach Chief's father to sell their land so that the government can build a hydroelectric dam in its place. It is the woman in the group, a woman who reminds Chief of Nurse Ratched, who determined they should avoid Chief's father and go directly to his mother. The woman reasoned that, because he took his white wife's name, Chief's mother will actually bear more influence on her husband's decision to sell the land. She told her comrades, "As my sociology professor used to emphasize, 'There is generally one person in every situation you must never underestimate the power of.'"

That night in the hospital ward, Chief awakens to hear McMurphy talking to an aide who is scraping gum from the bottom of Chief's bed. This inspires McMurphy to sing "Does Your Chewing Gum Lose Its Flavor on the Bedpost Overnight?" after the aide exits. This song causes Chief to laugh, indicating to McMurphy that he can hear. McMurphy offers a stick of Juicy Fruit to Chief and the Indian utters the words, "Thank you."

His ability to speak causes Chief to tell his life story to McMurphy. He says that his father's name was Tee Ah Millatoona, which means "The-Pine-that-Stands-Tallest-on-the-Mountain." He says that his white mother began at 5'9" tall but eventually grew bigger than Chief or his father together. Chief says that his mother and the Combine worked on his father to conform because he was physically large and did as he pleased—comparing him to McMurphy.

Chief tells McMurphy that eventually the Combine caused his father to sell the tribal lands and waterfalls. His father wound up a destitute alcoholic. He warns McMurphy that the Combine will work on McMurphy as well, because it believes he's too big.

The two men agree that McMurphy will pay for Chief to go on the fishing trip if Chief will lift the control panel that physically stymied McMurphy in Part 1. McMurphy begins to build Chief's self image, telling him that he has grown "half a foot already."

Commentary

McMurphy's positive impact on the patients continues to increase, prompting them to think more of themselves, as well as to question Nurse Ratched's arbitrary and abusive authority. For example, Chief's first utterances indicate a willingness to overcome his oppressive paranoia and engage himself communicatively with McMurphy. In addition,

Chief, to his amazement, is able to recall details of his childhood for the first time in years. These memories recount when he first felt ignored, indicating to the reader that Chief has pinpointed the source or cause of his illness and, by extension, knows that he can be cured.

The control panel that McMurphy wants Chief to lift is significant. The panel represents one thing that McMurphy is incapable of achieving, as outlined in Part 1 when he loses a bet trying to lift it. That fact that Chief can lift it reveals that he is regaining his physical confidence, but because he'll lift it as part of McMurphy's attempt to win a bet against the other patients by tricking them foreshadows McMurphy's downfall.

Chief's observation of McMurphy's tattoo also is revelatory in that it depicts the "dead man's hand" of aces and eights, the poker hand that Wild Bill Hickok was holding when he was shot to death.

Part 3
Two Whores

Summary

The day of the fishing trip, Chief refuses to sweep the floor for the African-American aides. McMurphy enlists Rub-a-Dub George, a cleanliness-obsessed Swedish sailor and fisherman, in the crew. When Candy Starr appears without her friend to pick up the patients for their excursion, Nurse Ratched announces that they can't go because there isn't enough room in one vehicle for all the patients. McMurphy talks Doctor Spivey into driving his own car. Spivey consents, partially because of his physical attraction to the alluringly attired Starr.

The group stops at a gasoline station on their way to the docks where they are treated rudely by the station attendants. McMurphy intervenes and the group is invigorated, a feeling that quickly evaporates when they reach the docks. Fishermen at the docks make negative comments about the patients and lewd remarks to Starr. The group, separated from McMurphy, make no effort to defend themselves or Starr from the rude behavior. The boat captain refuses to rent the boat to McMurphy because proper legal waivers weren't filled out. Frustrated, McMurphy gives the captain a bogus phone number and, while the captain makes a phone call, loads the boat and heads out to sea with the group.

McMurphy takes Starr below deck for a sexual interlude, and the group takes turns fishing. Before long, they are upon a school of fish and are bringing in salmon. The pandemonium that ensues resolves itself in the group engaged in the regenerative act of unabashed laughter. Spivey lands a huge flounder, which takes him more than an hour to bring on board. This causes the group to experience rough waters on their way back to dock. When they notice that there aren't enough life-jackets for the entire group, Chief notices that McMurphy wears one anyway.

When they return, their prodigious catch earns them the respect of the fisherman at the dock. The change in the patients is apparent to everyone: "these weren't the same bunch of weak-knees from a nuthouse that they'd watched take their insults on the dock this morning."

Driving back to the hospital, McMurphy convinces the group to drive by one of his boyhood homes. Chief notices that McMurphy is acting tired beyond the exertions of the day's excursion while McMurphy relates a lurid tale of losing his virginity when he was ten years old to a girl the same age or younger. While he relates further stories of barroom fights and sexual conquests, Chief recognizes a frantic look on McMurphy's face, "like there wasn't time left for something he had to do..."

Commentary

For the patients' morale, the fishing trip is a resounding success. The group starts out by mimicking McMurphy's bravado after the encounters with the surly gas station attendants, but reverts to their weaker selves when confronted by the fishermen at the boating dock. After removing themselves from the mainland, however, the group finds their respective footing through camaraderie, laughter, fishing, and the company of a woman who isn't a "ball-cutter."

The strain of improving the morale of his fellow patients begins to show on McMurphy, however. He begins to fear for his life, which is displayed when he chooses a life jacket for himself even though there aren't enough for the entire group. On the car ride back to the hospital, he tells a horrible story with a forced bravado that betrays his fatigue. Chief, watching McMurphy's face in the intermittent light of oncoming vehicles, notices that his hero's expression is frantic.

The religious imagery becomes much more apparent in this section as well. The character of Ellis, who is introduced as posing as if crucified in Part 1, tells the group that they are to be "fishers of men," which is the same instructions Jesus Christ gave his apostles. Christ's twelve apostles are echoed by Kesey's use of twelve group members who accompany McMurphy on the fishing trip.

Glossary

wheedle   to influence or persuade (a person) by flattery, soothing words, coaxing, and so on.

jounce   to shake, jolt, or bounce, as in riding.

flophouse   a very cheap hotel frequented chiefly by indigents.

keelhaul   to haul (a person) down through the water on one side of a ship, under the keel, and up on the other side as a punishment or torture.

troll   to fish with bait or a lure trailed on a line behind a slowly moving boat.

gaff   a spar or pole extending from the aft side of a mast and supporting a fore-and-aft sail.

jetty   a kind of wall built out into the water to restrain currents, protect a harbor or pier, and so on.

Part 4
The Big Nurse

Summary

The fourth and final section of this novel depicts the final show-down between Randle Patrick McMurphy and Nurse Ratched. This part begins with Chief telling the reader that Ratched began planning a counterattack on McMurphy while he and the group were on their fishing excursion. Chief somewhat omnisciently relates that Ratched knows that people eventually grow suspicious of individuals who seemingly operate selflessly on behalf of others.

She plants the seeds of dissent in the group while McMurphy takes a phone call. She prompts the group to question McMurphy's motive when she tells them he has won more than $300 from the other patients. While the patients enjoy the additional benefits that McMurphy has provided, they suspect that he may be motivated by more than philanthropic impulses.

Ratched manipulates the conversation by asking if any member of the group considers McMurphy a "martyr or a saint." She continues that McMurphy is taking credit for giving the patients items and freedoms that were not his to give. She climaxes her attack on McMurphy by revealing to the patients that McMurphy made money off the patients when he arranged the fishing trip. Ratched tells Billy Bibbit, McMurphy's most staunch defender, that she doesn't disapprove of McMurphy's actions, but that she feels the patients shouldn't delude themselves that McMurphy's actions are selfless.

After the meeting, Harding explains to the group that McMurphy is an example of American entrepreneurialism and would be embarrassed if he thought others claimed his motives were pure. He calls McMurphy "a sharp operator, level-headed as they come," and adds that "everything he's done was done with reason."

Bibbit disagrees with Harding, telling him that McMurphy couldn't possibly harbor ulterior motives in teaching Bibbit how to dance. Chief says that he and Bibbit are the only patients who believe in

McMurphy. McMurphy then appears and asks Bibbit to send money to Candy Starr so that she can visit. When Bibbit says that the ten dollars McMurphy tells him to send Starr is more than bus fare usually costs, McMurphy admits that he has asked Starr to bring alcohol when she visits.

In private, McMurphy asks Chief to lift the control panel. When Chief shows him that he can perform the task, McMurphy baits the group into a bet that pays five to one that no one can lift the panel. Learning that Ratched has ordered delousing showers for all the patients returned from the fishing trip, Chief says he wishes he could take the shower instead of lifting the panel. He feels that he's helping McMurphy cheat his friends out of their money. He performs the feat anyway and leaves the room in disgust.

McMurphy follows Chief to give him five dollars. He asks Chief why all the patients are treating him suspiciously. Chief responds that it's because McMurphy always appears to be winning things. McMurphy responds wearily, "Winning, for Christsakes.... Hoo boy, winning."

The group is led to the showers for delousing. The members taunt the African-American aides by making wisecracks and breaking wind. All is jovial until the aide Washington begins to harass Rub-a-Dub George, who is obsessed with cleanliness but never uses soap. As George becomes more upset at Washington's claims that he is infested with bugs, McMurphy steps in to defend George. Calling Washington several negative sexual and racial epithets, McMurphy shoves Washington away from George. Washington, still angry with McMurphy for bloodying his nose in the basketball game, strikes him.

Noting that McMurphy's voice reveals a "helpless, cornered despair," Chief relates the details of the ensuing fight. The aides outnumber McMurphy until Chief assists him. After they win the fight, McMurphy and Chief are handcuffed and led to the Disturbed Ward.

Commentary

McMurphy's motives are questioned by the group, prompted by the ideas planted by Nurse Ratched. Their suspicions are confirmed, however, when McMurphy asks Bibbit for extra money to pay for Starr's visit, and he tricks the patients into betting that Chief can't lift the control panel. The patients' perception that McMurphy is always "winning" eventually leads to McMurphy's downfall.

Character Insight

McMurphy's response to Chief's comment that he's always winning indicates that his rebellious behavior is taking its toll on McMurphy, which is underscored by his defending George from Washington in the showers.

McMurphy physically defends George, knowing that the other aides will come to Washington's assistance. Describing the "helpless, cornered despair in McMurphy's voice," Chief indicates that McMurphy is trapped into defending George and has no choice.

Glossary

vermin   various insects, bugs, or small animals regarded as pests because they are destructive, disease-carrying, and so on, as flies, lice, rats, or weasels.

Part 4
Up on Disturbed

Summary

McMurphy apologizes to Chief for getting him involved in the fight as the two are led to electroshock therapy. Alluding to his stay in a Chinese prison camp in the Korean War, McMurphy refuses to cooperate with Ratched to prevent the electroshock. Emulating the crucifixion, McMurphy lies down on the electroshock table and asks for a crown of thorns.

As Chief recovers from his electroshock, he remembers his mother's emasculating behavior toward him and his father. She civilizes them by forcing them to take her last name, Bromden, and moving them to town where "getting a Social Security card [is] a lot easier." He recites the nursery rhyme from which the book takes its title, a game called Tingle Tingle Tangle Toes. In the game, Mrs. Tingle Tangle Toes catches hens and puts them into pens while a goose flies overhead looking to pluck one of the hens out. Chief awakens soaked in his own urine in the Seclusion Room. He says he knows he has the aides beat this time.

Commentary

McMurphy enters the Disturbed Ward as a swaggering, drawling cowboy hero who even spits one of his teeth five feet into a metal wastebasket. Resigned to his eventual fate, he adopts the two-dimensional persona of the Western hero to continue his encouragement of the other patients, most notably Chief.

Literary Device

As Chief and McMurphy recover from electroshock, they hear a patient screaming, "I'm starting to spin, Indian," which reminds the reader that McMurphy's initials—RPM—are also the acronym for "revolutions per minute." Chief falls asleep "plagued by a hundred faces" like the screaming patient. He wonders how McMurphy can sleep, because Chief figures that McMurphy must see twice as many, if not thousands of faces. Chief describes the faces as exhibiting a "starved need...wanting things...asking things." From this, the reader

Style & Language

may draw further comparisons with Christ, who redeemed the world's sinners. Other religious imagery in this section includes McMurphy requesting a crown of thorns and anointing his temples with the conductor before receiving his electroshock.

This section of the novel is also notable for its inclusion of the Japanese nurse. This nurse disapproves of Nurse Ratched's methods, yet is not a woman of easy virtue. Her character displays that Kesey's depictions of women in the novel are not entirely misogynistic.

Character Insight

Interestingly, the electroshock jars loose further memories from Chief. He recalls air raids from his Army tenure and other events back further in his childhood. He remembers his mother refused to take her husband's Indian name. Instead, she tells him, "We ain't Indians. We're civilized and you remember it." Later, Chief is led back to the ward where he perceives a light fog produced by the Combine, but refuses to "slip off and hide in it. No...never again..." He tells the reader that he knows "this time I had them beat," indicating that his cure is nearly complete.

Part 4
There Had Been Times

Summary

McMurphy is given three more electroshock treatments, but his rebellious behavior continues while he is assigned to the Disturbed Ward. He declares that the treatments serve to recharge his batteries. He even goes so far as to pinch Ratched's behind. Chief recognizes, however, that McMurphy's stoicism falters whenever he hears his name called for another treatment.

McMurphy's absence from the ward, however, is serving to increase his legend among Harding, Scanlon, Bibbit, and the others. Realizing this, Ratched makes plans to bring McMurphy back to the ward. Fearing that she'll make an example out of McMurphy by keeping him in an electroshock-induced stupor, the patients devise an escape plot for him.

When McMurphy returns, he rejects the escape plan because he wants to be present when Starr visits for the express purpose of relieving Bibbit of his virginity.

During the next group meeting, Ratched suggests to Doctor Spivey that perhaps more drastic measures are required to curtail McMurphy's aggressive tendencies. She suggests an operation, which prompts McMurphy to ask, "There's no cause to do any cuttin', now, has there?" Not realizing he's talking about castration, Ratched begins to respond that the new procedure for lobotomies doesn't require cutting. When she realizes he's talking about his testicles in an attempt to make fun of her, she stops smiling.

McMurphy bribes the elderly African-American night watchman, Turkle, to allow Starr and her friend, Sandy, to enter the ward. The two women bring ample amounts of alcohol with them and, combined with Turkle's marijuana, the ward denizens throw a party. Sefelt experiences sex with Sandy while in the throes of an epileptic seizure. Sandy says, "Never in my life experienced anything to come even *halfway* near it." The remaining patients get drunk, and Bibbit retires to the Seclusion Room to have sex with Starr.

McMurphy and Harding discuss Harding's voluntary incarceration at the hospital, and Harding indicates that he's "different," presumably homosexual. McMurphy responds that all individuals are different but not all individuals feel it necessary to seek psychiatric care. The men make plans to allow McMurphy time to sleep before he escapes with Starr and Sandy. McMurphy and Sandy go to bed "more like two tired little kids than a grown man and a grown woman in bed together to make love." No one wakes up in time, and the African-American aides discover the debauchery when they arrive in the morning.

Commentary

McMurphy's demeanor is reflected in the actions of his fellow patients. Harding is the first to push his luck with Nurse Ratched, ribbing her that the patients have heard that McMurphy pinched her posterior region.

Chief reminisces about a conversation he overheard between Bibbit and Bibbit's mother, an emasculating woman intent on keeping her 31-year-old son a dependent child upon her. The conversation as related by Chief includes very heavy Oedipal overtones, which Bibbit seems to be overcoming as he nears the impending loss of his virginity to Starr.

Character Insight

During the debauchery of the ward party, Harding reveals to McMurphy that he has known his whole life that he is "shall we be kind and say different," indicating that he knows that he is a homosexual. Lack of social acceptance of homosexuals, believes Harding, caused him to go "crazy." He now feels that he is almost ready to rejoin society and accept himself. He credits McMurphy for his recovery, but notes that it has cost McMurphy his own sanity.

Part 4
I've Given What Happened Next

Summary

Nurse Ratched arrives and discovers that Bibbit and Starr have had sex. Bibbit blames Starr, the other patients for teasing him and, finally, McMurphy for his actions. Ratched threatens to tell Bibbit's mother and sends him to wait in Doctor Spivey's office where he commits suicide by cutting his neck.

Ratched blames McMurphy for the suicides of Bibbit and Cheswick, and he responds by physically attacking her after smashing through a glass door. He tears her uniform, exposing her ample bosom, and chokes her before being stopped by a group of aides, doctors, and nurses. He is sent to Disturbed, where he receives a lobotomy.

Several of the patients check themselves out before McMurphy is returned to the ward. When he does return, his friends deny that the lobotomized individual is McMurphy. Knowing that it is indeed McMurphy, Chief suffocates him and picks up the control panel to push out the screened window. Chief escapes, following the same path he saw the dog chase the geese. He takes a ride with a Mexican hauling sheep and decides to head back to visit the dam where his tribe once lived.

Commentary

Literary Device

Bibbit's betrayal of McMurphy and subsequent suicide has literary antecedents in the story of Judas, the apostle who betrayed Jesus Christ to the Roman soldiers and then hung himself. McMurphy's love for Bibbit induces him to attack Ratched after she accuses him of responsibility for his death. In his attack, McMurphy rips her uniform and exposes her large breasts. By exposing her as a human woman beneath her air of authority and starched uniforms, he robs her of her mechanical power, a symbolic act that frees the remaining patients to leave the hospital.

Literary Device

Because he is a Chronic and not free to leave the hospital at will, Chief escapes from the hospital. The path he takes, however, is the same path that he saw the dog chase the geese earlier in the novel. In the first scene, the dog runs toward the headlights of an oncoming car, which may be interpreted as a battle between animal and machine that the animal cannot possibly win. The reader is left wondering if Chief remains outside the hospital, or returns where he writes down his memories of McMurphy.

Glossary

hallucinate   to perceive sights, sounds, and so on that are not actually present.

lobotomy   a surgical operation in which a lobe of the brain, especially the frontal lobe of the cerebrum, is cut into or across as a treatment for psychosis.

ramshackle   loose and rickety; likely to fall to pieces; shaky.

CHARACTER ANALYSES

Randle Patrick McMurphy

Randle Patrick McMurphy is a red-haired, wild American of Irish descent. He unself-consciously engages in brawling, gambling, chicanery, and exercising his carnal nature. His primitive inclinations mark him as an iconoclast in a world that increasingly values conformity. His anti-authoritarian attitude has already caused him a dishonorable discharge from the U.S. Marines, a punishment subsequent to his leading a successful escape from a Chinese prisoner-of-war camp during the Korean War.

McMurphy is interred at the hospital for "diagnosis and possible treatment," reads Nurse Ratched, who continues: "Thirty-five years old. Never married. Distinguished Service Cross in Korea, for leading an escape from a Communist prison camp. A dishonorable discharge, afterward, for insubordination. Followed by a history of street brawls and barroom fights and a series of arrests for Drunkenness, Assault and Battery, Disturbing the Peace, *repeated* gambling, and one arrest—for Rape."

It is perhaps part of McMurphy's innate nature that he does not adhere to social strictures. It is also reasonable to assert that his imprisonment during the Korean conflict deeply impacted his distrust of authority. The fact that he was awarded the Distinguished Service Cross for leading an escape serves as a foreshadowing of events later in the novel, but could also serve to create a more complete understanding of his character's motivations.

Although not foreign to hard physical labor, McMurphy chafes at his assignment to a prison work farm and looks forward to his confinement to a mental hospital as a pleasant way to spend the rest of his sentence for brawling. The violence of fighting is as natural an activity for men in a natural state as is the desire for sexual relations. McMurphy's run-ins with the law for statutory rape he declares preposterous, as his fifteen-year-old female "victim" lied about her age and initiated the sexual interlude.

Upon his arrival at the hospital, McMurphy encounters Dale Harding, identified as the "bull-goose loony." The interaction between the two presents an interesting contrast between the salt-of-the-earth, everyman philosophy of McMurphy and the more intellectualized, academic, and effete point-of-view of Harding. Harding's abstract arguments in defense of Ratched are easily defeated by McMurphy's empirical observations of her manipulations of the men in the ward.

McMurphy observes that Ratched's tactics are intended more to ensure her authority than benefit the patients, and that the most glaring example of this tactic is using the men to spy and report on each other. The other men realize that McMurphy is correct, and begin to dedicate their admiration and allegiance to him. When McMurphy restrains from questioning Ratched in an attempt to appease her and thus expedite his release, the men, particularly Cheswick, see it as a betrayal. Cheswick's subsequent suicide and McMurphy's introduction to the castrating wife of Harding serve to convince McMurphy that he is the leader, albeit reluctant, of another escape. This escape is not from a Communist POW camp, however. McMurphy must assist the men that need to escape the conforming attitudes and restrictions that society is imposing on them.

McMurphy increasingly becomes identified with Christ, from the crucifixion on the electroshock therapy table preceded by the patient "washing his hands of the whole affair" to the echoes of the Last Supper when Billy Bibbit engages in sexual relations with Candy Starr. Like Christ, McMurphy sacrifices himself for the benefit of the group, and in doing so, he loses his free will. Chief makes it clear that McMurphy is not acting on his own when he brutally attacks Ratched, but in accordance with the wills of the other patients.

The continued references to McMurphy's tired appearance also point up the effects of his sacrifices for the patients. Harding explains to McMurphy that he has helped them regain their sanity at the risk of losing his own. McMurphy has ceased to be himself and is being forced to be what the others think he is. They can recognize themselves only through him, and he must continue to give them something to emulate.

The name Randle Patrick McMurphy forms the acronym "RPM," which is also the acronym for "Revolutions Per Minute"—the measurement for the speed at which a phonograph record is played. Like the phonograph record, McMurphy is a whirling dervish; yet a man also being "played" by the Combine, destined to spin around and around without ever reaching a worthwhile destination.

Nurse Ratched

In literary terms, Nurse Ratched is a flat character, which means she encounters no changes whatsoever throughout the book. She begins as a scheming, manipulative agent of the Combine and remains so at the novel's conclusion. Her depiction resembles the villains of comic books and one-reel film serials in that she asserts arbitrary control simply because she can.

Much of Ratched's character is evident in her name. McMurphy pronounces it "Rat-shed" during an early section of the novel, indicating that she possesses rodent-like qualities of working quietly, quickly, and to the disadvantage of her victims. The reader is reminded that rats were the carriers of the Black Plague during the Middle Ages, and Ratched infects the hospital's orderlies, student nurses, public relations personnel, and patients with her irrational desire for order.

The name Ratched is also a pun of "ratchet," which is a both a verb and a noun for a device that uses a twisting motion to tighten bolts into place. This pun serves a greater metaphorical purpose in Kesey's hands, as Ratched manipulates the patients and twists them to spy on one another or expose each others' weaknesses in group sessions. The ratchet, as critic Ronald Wallace notes, is also "like a ratchet wrench she keeps her patients 'adjusted,' but like a ratchet, a gear in the Combine, she is herself mechanically enmeshed." The most comic reading of her name, however, is as a pun on the word "wretched."

As Chief describes Ratched, she "tends to get real put out if something keeps her outfit from running like a smooth, accurate, precision-made machine. The slightest thing messy or out of kilter or in the way ties her into a little white knot of tight-smiled fury." Chief goes on to describe her as resembling a doll on the outside, but mechanized and steel underneath. Her expressions are always "calculated and mechanical."

The Public Relations man depicts Ratched as "just like a mother," and in terms of such emasculating mothers as Mrs. Bibbit and Mary Louise Bromden elsewhere in the book, this is clearly not meant by Kesey to be a compliment. Indeed, Ratched also emasculates the men on the ward, forcing them to feel like misbehaving little boys, to reveal each others' secrets and to scare them from ever challenging her authority. But she hides her gender from the world by obscuring her large breasts as much as possible behind the sterility of a starched white nurse's uniform.

Chief Bromden

Because he is the narrator, the reader knows more about Chief than any of the novel's other characters. The book takes its title from a nursery rhyme Chief learned from his Native American grandmother. His heritage aligns Chief with the natural world, a world that his white mother conspired to destroy when she influenced Chief's father to sell his tribal lands. This sale enabled the construction of a hydroelectric dam on the Columbia River, representing Chief's first experience of the victory of mechanization over the natural world. He remembers that his mother kept getting "bigger" while his father "shrunk" into alcoholism and despair. Insult is added to injury when Chief is forced to adopt his mother's white name, Bromden, rather than his father's Indian name.

Chief played high school football, which enabled him to travel to different areas. During one out-of-town trip, his team is given a tour of a factory where he meets a young African-American woman who begs him to take her away with him.

Fully grown to 6'7", Chief enters the Army during World War II. In the Army he learns about the electronics that he will later schizophrenically hallucinate as part of the Combine. The Combine is the invention of Chief's paranoia; a large mechanized matrix that enforces its control over humankind by making it conform to rigid standards of behavior. Chief believes he can hear the mechanized gears of the Combine behind the walls and beneath the floors of the hospital where he has been living as a deaf-mute since the war.

As the novel progresses, Chief's delusions decrease. He no longer witnesses the fog that the Combine would regularly emit on the ward, and he even begins to communicate verbally with McMurphy and the other ward patients. A strong man who doubts his own powers, Chief's confidence is returned by McMurphy's program to "blow" the deflated Chief back up. His salvation is completed when he performs a mercy killing on the lobotomized McMurphy and escapes from the hospital. The victory of his escape, however, is undermined by the novel's first chapter in which the Chief appears to be telling the story from the hospital ward. "But it's all the truth even if it didn't happen," he writes, leading the reader to doubt the success of McMurphy's rebellion.

Dale Harding

An intelligent, educated, and effeminate man, Harding is initially set up as McMurphy's foil. He exists totally within the realm of his mind whereas McMurphy represents a natural man. Harding chooses to lead his life as an individual repressing his homosexual urges while suffering the humiliation of never fully pleasing his promiscuously unfaithful wife. Nurse Ratched seems pleased to remind the group that "his wife's ample bosom at times gives him a feeling of inferiority," while Chief describes him as "a wild, jerky puppet doing a high-strung dance."

Despite his weakness, Harding is the first patient to acknowledge to McMurphy that the patients "are victims of a matriarchy." He also becomes McMurphy's most ardent supporter, defending him against Ratched's assertion that McMurphy acts only out of self-interest. In McMurphy's absence, Harding takes over leadership responsibilities by adopting McMurphy's mannerisms and behavior. After the party, Harding is among the first patients to leave the hospital.

Billy Bibbit

Because of the virginity he retains until he is more than 30 years old, Bibbit is perhaps the most repressed member of the group. His mother employs Oedipal tactics to keep Bibbit attached to her. This woman also maintains a close relationship with Nurse Ratched, a relationship crucial to the outcome of the novel.

Bibbit behaves in an adolescent fashion at the beginning of the novel, giggling into his hand at prurient remarks and writing down his observations concerning members of the group in Ratched's book. His ineffectuality is underscored by the scars on his wrists from an unsuccessful suicide attempt made when his mother forced him to break off an engagement with a woman she felt was socially beneath her son.

Bibbit eventually comes to idolize McMurphy, who is only four years his senior. McMurphy arranges for Bibbit to lose his virginity to Candy Starr, initiating the chain of events that causes Bibbit's suicide and McMurphy's lobotomy and subsequent murder. While still susceptible to Ratched's manipulations, Bibbit nevertheless finds the strength to succeed in killing himself in defiance of her authority and as penance for betraying McMurphy. It is telling that Bibbit succeeds by cutting his own throat when he was previously unable to succeed in the more simple task of cutting his wrists.

CRITICAL
ESSAYS

The Role of Women

The female characters in *One Flew Over the Cuckoo's Nest* can be divided into two extreme categories: "ball-cutters" and whores. The former is represented by Nurse Ratched, Harding's wife, Billy Bibbit's mother, and Chief Bromden's mother.

Each of these women are intent on dominating men by emasculating them, whereas the whores Candy and Sandy are dedicated to pleasuring men and doing what they're told. Despite the obvious nature of this observation, Kesey aims higher than asserting male dominance over female acquiescence. His goal is to assert those qualities identified as feminine to undermine those qualities considered masculine.

In between the two female extremes of ball-cutter and whore is the Asian-American nurse in the Disturbed Ward who bandages McMurphy. She represents an ideal middle ground—a compassionate, intelligent, nurturing woman who is nevertheless powerless to save McMurphy. McMurphy flirts with her after she relates Ratched's history to him. She doesn't succumb to his advances, presumably to display that Kesey realizes that women are more than sexual playthings. Her presence in the novel is short-lived, however, and McMurphy is quickly returned to the machinations of Nurse Ratched.

"We are victims of a matriarchy here," Harding acknowledges to McMurphy after McMurphy characterizes his first group therapy meeting as "a pecking party." When Harding protests that Ratched is "not some kind of giant monster of the poultry clan, bent on sadistically pecking out our eyes," McMurphy responds, "No buddy, not that. She ain't pecking at your *eyes*. That's not what she's peckin' at."

However, McMurphy acknowledges that not all ball-cutters are women when he continues: "No, that nurse ain't some kinda monster chicken, buddy, what she is is a ball-cutter. I've seen a thousand of 'em, old and young, men and women. Seen 'em all over the country and in the homes—people who try to make you weak so they can get you to toe the line, to follow their rules, to live like they want you to. And the best way to do this, to get you to knuckle under, is to weaken you by gettin' you where it hurts the worst."

By polarizing the battle between repression and freedom as a battle between feminization and masculinity, machinery versus nature, and civilized versus wild, Kesey offers a simplified mythology much like the comic book heroes he reveres. The war isn't between the sexes, but an archetypal battle between the more positive masculine qualities and the more negative feminine qualities. This motif suits his purpose because it allows Kesey to express a worldview of good against evil in which one of the cardinal virtues of McMurphy's world is masculinity. It is the masculine virtue that engenders nature, spontaneity, sexual freedom, and rebellion against the feminine qualities of societal repression under the guise of civilization.

Of the antagonistic women in the book, the reader learns most about Nurse Ratched and Chief Bromden's mother. Chief's observations of her on the ward illustrate Nurse Ratched, but the reader knows more about the castration of husband and son through the depiction of Chief's mother.

It is through Mrs. Bromden that the government gains rights to the Indian land on which the dam is built. Two white men and a woman come to speak to the Chief's father, but the woman realizes that the better approach is to speak first with Chief's white mother.

Once Chief's mother convinces her husband to sell the land in order for her to return to civilization, both husband and son begin to lose their identities. Chief relates that his father begins to "shrink" in size after taking his wife's last name as his own: "You're the biggest by God fool if you think that a good Christian woman takes on a name like Tee Ah Millatoona. You were born into a name, so okay, I'm born into a name. Bromden. Mary Louise Bromden."

Adopting the mother's name is a mark of an ultimate sacrifice Chief's father makes to appease his wife, losing in turn his own pride and self-sufficiency. Father and son are forced to adopt the white person's name and lose all that Tee Ah Millatoona (meaning the Pine-That-Stands-Tallest-on-the-Mountain) symbolizes. The result is the alcoholism and death of the father and the institutionalization of the son.

The Film and the Novel

While retaining many of the novel's themes and motifs, the filmed version of *One Flew Over the Cuckoo's Nest* differs in several significant ways. The film, released in 1975, won Academy Awards for Best Picture, Best Actor (Jack Nicholson), Best Actress (Louise Fletcher), Best Screenplay Adapted from Other Material (Lawrence Hauben and Bo Goldman), and Best Director (Milos Forman). Since its release, the film has been certified as one of the Top 100 American Films by the American Film Institute.

The film is also noted for its casting, which includes early cinematic appearances by such later respected actors as Brad Dourif (Billy Bibbit), Christopher Lloyd (Taber), and Danny DeVito (Martini). Other actors include real hospital superintendent Dr. Dean Brooks (Doctor Spivey), Will Sampson (Chief Bromden), Sydney Lassick (Charlie Cheswick), Marya Small (Candy Starr), and William Redfield (Dale Harding).

The most notable difference between the film and the novel is the story's point of view. In the novel, Chief Bromden is the narrator who reveals the story of the battle of wills between Nurse Ratched and Randle Patrick McMurphy. In fact, Chief arguably is the novel's hero who undergoes the most notable changes in the novel. While detailing the events in the mental institution, Chief reveals biographical information of his own life before his institutionalization. We learn that Chief is a paranoid schizophrenic, a war veteran, and a half-breed Indian whose white mother conspired with the U.S. government to emasculate his proud father, an American Indian whose name Tee Ah Millatoona translates as "Pine-That-Stands-Tallest-on-the-Mountain."

The filmed version discards Chief as the story's narrator, discards the background story of Chief, and relegates his character to a secondary—albeit important—character to McMurphy. In the film, McMurphy is clearly the hero.

Chief's delusional episodes of witnessing the inner workings of the Combine and its fog machines are eliminated in the film in favor of scenes written that omnisciently expand on McMurphy's character and his background, as well as expand on his charitable nature.

In addition, Chief eventually becomes fully communicative in the novel while muttering only one phrase—"Juicy Fruit"—in the film. This explains how McMurphy is able to bring Chief along on the fishing excursion in the novel, a detail not explained in the film.

The film also softens McMurphy's more objectionable behavior in the book. Instead, he becomes more of a roguish con man than an unpredictably fearsome individual prone to bursts of physical violence against others to achieve his ends. Also missing from the film are several key symbolic elements, including McMurphy's poker-hand tattoo that foreshadows his death. The tattoo depicts aces and eights, known as the dead-man's hand in accordance to the legend of the poker hand held by Wild Bill Hickock when he was murdered.

In the film, McMurphy boasts that he was conned into statutory rape by a teenaged girl who lied about her age. "But Doc, she was fifteen years old, going on thirty-five, Doc, and, uh, she told me she was eighteen and she was, uh, very willing, you know what I mean," Nicholson's McMurphy asserts. "I practically had to take to sewin' my pants shut. But, uh between you and me, uh, she might have been fifteen, but when you get that little red beaver right up there in front of ya, I don't think it's crazy at all now and I don't think you do either. No man alive could resist that, and that's why I got into jail to begin with. And now they're telling me I'm crazy over here because I don't sit there like a goddamn vegetable. Don't make a bit of sense to me. If that's what's bein' crazy is, then I'm senseless, out of it, gone-down-the-road, wacko. But no more, no less, that's it."

In the novel, McMurphy's boasts of being seduced by a nine-year-old girl are related with a sense of false bravado and world-weariness. His initial incarceration isn't for statutory rape, it's for being "a guy who fights too much and fucks too much." In the novel, McMurphy freely admits to conning his fellow patients for his own financial gain. The film only shows McMurphy winning cigarettes from his comrades.

Certain critical scenes from the novel are eliminated in the cinematic version. Of these, the suicide of Cheswick, is most notable. Cheswick's character was the first individual in the novel to receive invigoration from McMurphy's antics. When McMurphy decides to toe the line—that is, conform to Nurse Ratched's wishes—it is after hearing from the swimming pool lifeguard that the length of their mutual confinements is entirely at the discretion of Nurse Ratched. It is in the same pool that Cheswick—feeling abandoned and betrayed by McMurphy's subsequent conformist behavior—chooses to drown himself.

One scene not in the film is McMurphy's final con against the Acutes. In the novel, McMurphy manipulates Chief Bromden to lift the control panel after McMurphy takes bets from the Acutes that it can't be done. McMurphy, of course, had already hedged his bet by having Chief display his ability to lift the panel previously. When Chief performs the trick for the Acutes, he feels used and betrayed by McMurphy. The film balances a scene of McMurphy unsuccessfully trying to lift a basin with the scene of Chief lifting it successfully and flinging it through the window while avoiding the scene of Chief lifting it to win a bet for McMurphy.

Another sequence in the film differs greatly from the novel. The fishing episode in the novel is a planned event that Nurse Ratched repeatedly attempts to sabotage. Despite this, McMurphy convinces Doctor Spivey to join the group when the alluring prostitute Candy arrives with only one car. In the filmed version, McMurphy hijacks a waiting institutional bus and instructs the film's principal male cast to participate in an act of rebellion. As a result, the scene at the gas station, when McMurphy confronts the surly and abusive attendants, temporarily empowers the patients, and Doctor Spivey is not depicted. Additionally missing is the scene when the group passively endures the jeers and taunts of the fishermen at the dock.

In the film, McMurphy's character remains the same roguish noncomformist up until his lobotomy. The book, however, details Chief's observations of McMurphy's short-lived attempt to conform to Nurse Ratched's rules and the other patients' distrust of McMurphy engendered by Nurse Ratched, as well as McMurphy's increasing sadness and sensing of his own withering strength and impending doom.

The film also differs from the novel in its depiction of the events leading to McMurphy's introduction to electroshock therapy. The novel carefully establishes a character not in the film, Big George. George's obsession with cleanliness is established prior to the fishing excursion, and becomes a pivotal plot element when Nurse Ratched orders the African-American orderly, Washington, to administer an enema to George in the shower. Washington's threatening behavior toward George prompts McMurphy to reluctantly challenge the orderly. The resulting melee is the impetus for Nurse Ratched to send McMurphy and his accomplice, Chief Bromden, to the Disturbed Ward, where they receive electroshock therapy. The film employs the initial altercation between McMurphy and Washington as the impetus for Nurse Ratched to send McMurphy, Chief, and Charlie Cheswick (who doesn't commit suicide in the film) to the Disturbed Ward.

Perhaps the most telling difference between the film and the novel is the ending. The novel contains an episode missing from the film wherein Chief observes a dog sniffing gopher holes from the hospital window. The dog is distracted by a flock of geese forming a cross against a full moon. The dog chases the geese toward a road where it is implied the dog will confront an automobile with the inevitably tragic result that machine will triumph over nature. Coincidentally, this is the same course the Chief follows when he escapes from the hospital, giving the novel's resolution a degree of uncertainty as to whether the Chief will succeed in the outside world or succumb to a worse fate in a world increasingly overrun by dehumanizing mechanization. The film's conclusion, however, depicts Chief running from the hospital toward what the viewer assumes is happiness and liberty.

Exhibiting pronounced differences from the novel, the film nonetheless retains the themes of natural versus institutional, the battle of creative nonconformity against arbitrary and autocratic authority, the redemptive qualities of unrepressed sexuality, and the desultory effects of unbalanced feminine dominance.

While the film is generally regarded a cinematic masterpiece, Ken Kesey has vowed he will never view it due to disputes with the film's producers, Michael Douglas and Saul Zaentz. Douglas's father, the actor Kirk Douglas, was the first actor to portray McMurphy in the 1960s stage version of the novel. Former Creedence Clearwater Revival singer-songwriter John Fogerty's perception of Zaentz's business practices, coincidentally, were the subject of a disparaging song and video entitled "Zaentz Can't Dance."

McMurphy as Comic Book Christ

One Flew Over the Cuckoo's Nest features many allusions and references to Christian religion. Most obvious is McMurphy's martyrdom at the novel's climax. But this incident is foreshadowed throughout the novel with a series of direct references to events recounted in the New Testament.

While McMurphy's actions and attitudes are at first glance more Dionysian than Christian in that he emphasizes gambling, womanizing, and drinking over spirituality, his messianic qualities are apparent from his initial entrance into the ward. His laughter—representative of the human spirit—is contrasted with the snickers the patients hide with their hands and the disingenuous laugh of the Public Relations man. The machinations of the Combine trap their spirit. McMurphy's laughter, however, is described by Chief Bromden as "free and loud and it comes out of his wide grinning mouth and spreads in rings bigger and bigger till it's lapping against the walls all over the ward.... This sounds real. I realize it's the first laugh I've heard in years."

Later, Chief describes McMurphy's laughter during the fishing excursion: "Rocking farther and farther backward against the cabin top, spreading his laugh out across the water—laughing at the girl, at the guys, at George, at me sucking my bleeding thumb, at the captain back at the pier and the bicycle rider and the service-station guys and the five thousand houses and the Big Nurse and all of it. Because he knows you have to laugh at the things that hurt you just to keep yourself in balance, just to keep the world from running you plumb crazy. He knows there's a painful side; he knows my thumb smarts and his girl friend has a bruised breast and the doctor is losing his glasses, but he won't let the pain blot out the humor no more'n he'll let the humor blot out the pain."

In the comic-book universe created by Kesey, life is polarized between pain and laughter, much like the Christian faith teaches that life is either sin or salvation. But as the Christian faith preaches that all humans are sinners capable of salvation, McMurphy instructs his disciples that life's miseries are redeemed through laughter, which is depicted as the ultimate rebellion.

The first blatant reference to Jesus Christ occurs when Chief introduces the Chronic patient Ellis. The recipient of many electroshock treatments, Ellis adopts a pose of crucifixion by spreading his arms against the wall, reflecting the shape of the electroshock table and directly alluding to Christ nailed to the cross. Chief reemphasizes this posture when he relates Harding's explanation of electroshock to McMurphy: "You are strapped to a table, shaped, ironically, like a cross, with a crown of electric sparks in place of thorns."

Later in the book, Ellis mimics Christ's instruction to his disciples when he tells Bibbit before leaving to fish to be a "fisher of men"—a phrase preceding the conversion from other religions to Christianity. It is perhaps a coincidence that Ellis's name is the phonetic spelling of the first two letters of the acronym for lysergic acid diethylamide (LSD), a synthetic psychotropic drug that sometimes results in religious delusions in those who ingest it. As noted previously, Kesey was among the civilian population that the U.S. government used for its human experiments of the drug.

The number of men accompanying McMurphy on the fishing excursion is twelve, just like the number of Christ's disciples. The bravado displayed by the patients following the gas station incident is revealed by Chief to be a bluff, much like the actions of Christ's disciples prior to his crucifixion. During the actual fishing, however, the patients embrace their identities while McMurphy retreats into the background. This sequence serves as a Pentecost of sorts as the patients finally embrace the spirit of McMurphy much like the Apostles were filled with the Holy Spirit following Christ's crucifixion. When the boat is lacking enough life jackets for everyone, McMurphy takes one for himself to allow the patients most in need of asserting their own individuality to go without.

Christ's sabbatical in the desert and triumphant return are reflected in McMurphy's period of playing it safe and toeing the line to appease Nurse Ratched. When McMurphy returns to his old self, he forces his hand through the window of the nurses' station, which can be taken either as a metaphor of Christ's clearing the merchants from the temple or his last vestige of human glory when he returns to Jerusalem on Palm Sunday.

Christ's trial and punishment is echoed when McMurphy and Chief are removed to the Disturbed Ward where a patient repeats the words of Christ's reluctant adjudicator, Pontius Pilate: "I wash my hands...." McMurphy lies down arms outspread on the table and refers to the administration of electroshock conductant as the anointing of his head with "a crown of thorns."

Any retelling of the New Testament Gospels, however, would not be complete without the inclusion of the Last Supper, a betrayal by a loyal follower, and death and resurrection. The party held in the ward resembles Christ's Last Supper complete with transubstantiated wine— a narcotic cough syrup spiked with vodka—and the Mary Magdalene-like presence of the two prostitutes Candy and Sandy. Bibbit's betrayal does not lie so much in his attempts to lay the blame for his sexual interlude with Candy on McMurphy as it does with his subsequent suicide. Judas committed suicide after betraying Christ to the Roman soldiers. Bibbit, on the other hand, betrays McMurphy by abandoning the spirit of rebellion and self-realization by killing himself out of fear of his mother's rapprochement.

Realizing that his efforts will be forgotten if he simply escapes after Bibbit's suicide, McMurphy attacks Ratched. This final, violent act— out of character with Christianity—is the sacrifice McMurphy makes to guarantee his martyrdom. Ratched cruelly lobotomizes him, relinquishing him of his very identity. Realizing this, Chief suffocates him, escapes, and lives to relate his gospel of the life and works of McMurphy.

As noted by critic Gary Carey, however, the parallels between Christ and McMurphy "should not be pushed too far," noting that their respective martyrdoms "have quite different meanings." While Christ died to redeem the sins of the individual, writes Carey, McMurphy's death is to save the patients from the sins society perpetrates against them.

Like the superheroes in comic books, McMurphy differs from Christ in that he weakens as his followers grow stronger. Indeed, McMurphy adopts the language of the B-movie cowboy or comic-book hero rather than a religious or even spiritual leader.

McMurphy's Cinematic Brothers in Rebellion

The character of Randle Patrick McMurphy shares many similarities with other cinematic figures of the past 50 years. A trip to your local video store or library where many of these videos are readily available will serve to elucidate the themes of rebellion against repression found in *One Flew Over the Cuckoo's Nest*. These works are often set in enclosed spaces, such as seagoing vessels and prisons, to present a small microcosm of humanity that contrasts rigid authority with the free-spirited nature of the works' respective protagonists.

Mr. Roberts

McMurphy's rebellious and messianic qualities and subsequent martyrdom resemble the character Mr. Roberts in the stage play and film adaptation of *Mr. Roberts*. In the film, Roberts (played by Henry Fonda) is assigned to a supply ship during World War II. Roberts longs to see battle in the South Pacific, but his captain (played by James Cagney) refuses to approve his transfer. The captain is a one-dimensional tyrant and is challenged continuously by Roberts.

Much like McMurphy, Roberts also experiences a period where he yields to the authority wielded by a tyrant. When Roberts finally receives his transfer, his rebellious spirit lives on in his replacement, Ensign Pulver (played by Jack Lemmon), who adopts the mantle of crew spokesperson upon hearing of Roberts' heroic death in battle.

Cool Hand Luke

While the similarities between Jesus Christ and Mr. Roberts are subtle, they are far more pronounced in the title character Paul Newman portrays in the film *Cool Hand Luke*. Sentenced to a chain gang for cutting the tops off a town's parking meters, Luke galvanizes his fellow prisoners by challenging them to join him in his thwarting the abusive authority of the warden (played by Strother Martin).

Much like the fishing excursion in *One Flew Over the Cuckoo's Nest* served to build the patients' allegiance to McMurphy, the characters in *Cool Hand Luke* come to revere Luke when he attempts to eat fifty raw eggs to win a bet. This results in the prisoners bonding together to assert their own humanity.

Elsewhere in the film, Luke endures prolonged solitary confinements to a box where he bakes in the hot Southern work farm sun, resembling Jesus Christ's forty days of fasting and prayer in the desert. A consistent visual motif displays Luke against images of a crucifix, especially the crossed roads on which the chain gang labors.

The Shawshank Redemption

Based upon a short story by Stephen King, the film *The Shawshank Redemption* is also set in a prison. The prisoners learn to reject fear and that "hope can set you free" through the examples set by the inmate Andy Dufresne (played by Tim Robbins). Among other things, Dufresne lobbies for a prison library that enables the prisoners to ennoble themselves with literature, classical music, and opera. In a much more secular vein, however, *The Shawshank Redemption* allows its protagonist to live after he escapes through ingenuous means.

Fight Club

The 1999 film *Fight Club* also bears many similarities to *One Flew Over the Cuckoo's Nest*. In the film, the characters Jack (played by Edward Norton) and Tyler Durden (played by Brad Pitt) rail against a society of rampant self-centeredness and consumerism. "Self improvement is masturbation," Durden tells Jack, a character formerly obsessed with the accumulation of designer brand furniture to fill the void of his otherwise meaningless existence.

In an effort to find sincerity and human connection, the healthy and unaddicted Jack attends various support groups and 12-step programs. He agrees with another "faker," a woman named Marla Singer (played by Helena Bonham Carter), that people actually listen to other people speak only when they think the speaker is terminally ill.

But these groups serve to weaken men further because they encourage a level of sensitivity that can only be described as feminine. Coincidentally, the group that Jack feels closest to is a collective of testicular cancer patients—men emasculated by disease and the removal of their testicles. The member of the group with the closest connection to Jack is Robert Paulsen (played by Meat Loaf), a former bodybuilder whose cancer was brought on by the use of steroids. Paulsen's treatment, however, has raised his body's estrogen level, causing him to grow breasts.

Durden's perception that contemporary American males have become increasingly more feminized as a result of being "a generation of men raised by women," also hearkens to McMurphy's attacks on "ball-cutters." Instead of marrying, Durden advises Jack to live life to its fullest by participating in rebellious acts, including graphic fights that enable the fighters to regain a semblance of masculinity. The mayhem perpetrated by Durden and his followers, however, quickly escalates into a fascistic, proletarian movement bent upon total societal annihilation.

CliffsNotes Review

Use this CliffsNotes Review to test your understanding of the original text, and reinforce what you've learned in this book. After you work through the review and essay questions, identify the quote section, and the fun and useful practice projects, you're well on your way to understanding a comprehensive and meaningful interpretation of Kesey's *One Flew Over the Cuckoo's Nest*.

Q&A

1. The control panel used by Chief Bromden to escape represents

    a. An overthrow of control

    b. His recovery from paranoid schizophrenia

    c. McMurphy's resurrection

2. Chief Bromden fakes muteness and deafness because

    a. It enables him to spy on Nurse Ratched and the aides

    b. He has grown accustomed to being ignored

    c. He fears that language cannot accurately convey human thoughts

3. McMurphy is a war hero who

    a. Led a group of escapees from a Korean War prison camp

    b. Commanded a submarine during World War II

    c. Led a successful raid against a North Vietnamese ammunitions dump in the Vietnam War

4. When Harding confesses to McMurphy that he's different, he means

    a. He is more intelligent than his wife and friends

    b. He is insane

    c. He is homosexual

5. Charles Cheswick commits suicide because

    a. He feels betrayed by McMurphy's conformity

    b. He discovers that Nurse Ratched won't sign his release

    c. He has learned that his wife is unfaithful

6. Doctor Spivey is controlled by Nurse Ratched because

   a. She knows he is addicted to morphine and she is blackmailing him

   b. She and his wife are good friends

   c. She provides him with morphine for his addiction

7. Billy Bibbit is in the hospital because

   a. His mother and Nurse Ratched are friends

   b. He is afraid of the opposite sex

   c. He has attempted suicide

8. What is the meaning of the recurring motif of the dog and the car?

Answers: (1) a. (2) b. (3) a. (4) c. (5) a. (6) a. (7) c. (8) The conflict between natural and mechanical forces.

Identify the Quote

1. "Geese up there, white man. You know it. Geese this year. And last year. And the year before and the year before."

2. "I don't deal blackjack so good, hobbled like this, but I maintain I'm a fire-eater in a stud game."

3. "We've simply been witness to the fading of his magnificent psychopathic suntan."

4. "And yet he seems to do things without thinking of himself at all, as if he were a martyr or a saint."

5. "Feet and inches? A guy at the carnival looked her over and says five feet nine and weighs a hundred and thirty pounds, but that was because he'd just *saw* her. She got bigger all the time."

Answers: (1) Chief Bromden's father speaking to the government officials negotiating the sale of tribal land in Part 1. (2) McMurphy to the Acutes upon returning from electroshock therapy in Part 4. (3) Dale Harding discussing the weakening McMurphy after the fishing excursion in Part 3. (4) Nurse Ratched to the group in McMurphy's absence in Part 4. (5) Chief Bromden discussing his mother during his first conversation with McMurphy in Part 3.

Essay Questions

1. How does the depiction of lobotomies and electroshock therapy differ in other works of literature and film?

2. Read Tom Wolfe's *The Electric Kool-Aid Acid Test*. Relate how the characters of Randle Patrick McMurphy and Chief Bromden resemble the real-life Ken Kesey and Neal Cassady.

3. Compare and contrast the similarities and differences between Jesus Christ and Randle Patrick McMurphy.

4. Trace references to machines throughout the book. Does the frequency with which they are mentioned as threatening correspond in any way with Chief's mental states?

5. Consider Nurse Ratched as a character, rather than a symbol. How much do we really know about her personality? Speculate about Kesey's views on the Women's Liberation movement.

6. Trace the Civil Rights Movement in the United States since the Civil War, and explore whether Kesey's treatment of African Americans in *One Flew Over the Cuckoo's Nest* is racist.

Practice Projects

1. Create a Web site to introduce *One Flew Over the Cuckoo's Nest* to other readers. Design pages to intrigue and inform your audience, and invite other readers to post their thoughts and responses to their reading of the novel.

2. Choose a scene from the novel and dramatize it for other classes. The production will require putting the scene in play form (freely adapting according to inspiration), assigning roles, directing, and staging the production. Follow the performance with a discussion of the novel's themes.

CliffsNotes Resource Center

The learning doesn't need to stop here. CliffsNotes Resource Center shows you the best of the best—links to the best information in print and online about the author and/or related works. And don't think that this is all we've prepared for you; we've put all kinds of pertinent information at www.cliffsnotes.com. Look for the terrific resources at your favorite bookstore or local library and on the Internet. When you're online, make your first stop www.cliffsnotes.com where you'll find more incredibly useful information about *One Flew Over the Cuckoo's Nest*.

Books

This CliffsNotes book provides a meaningful interpretation of *One Flew Over the Cuckoo's Nest* published by Wiley Publishing, Inc. If you are looking for information about the author and/or related works, check out these other publications:

One Flew Over the Cuckoo's Nest: Text and Criticism by Ken Kesey, contains a letter by Marcia L. Falk to the editor of *The New York Times*. Falk indicts Kesey and the stage adaptation of *One Flew Over the Cuckoo's Nest* for sexism, identifying all the play's female characters as demonized depictions of womanhood. Falk also argues that the text encourages white racism against African Americans and Native Americans. Edited by John Clark Pratt, Viking Press, 1973.

"The Higher Sentimentality," by Leslie A. Fiedler, recounts antecedents for the relationship between Chief Bromden and Randle Patrick McMurphy in Mark Twain's *Huckleberry Finn*. Fiedler also believes the novel belongs to an American genre begun with James Fenimore Cooper's *Leatherstocking* series and continuing through American comic books of the 1950s. Included in Fiedler's *The Return of the Vanishing American*, Stein and Day Publishers, 1968.

"What Laughter Can Do: Ken Kesey's One Flew Over the Cuckoo's Nest," by Ronald Wallace, defends the novel against charges of racism and sexism. Wallace believes the novel is both a romantic and comic novel. In *The Last Laugh: Form and Affirmation in the Contemporary American Comic Novel*, University of Missouri Press, 1979, pp. 90-114.

The Electric Kool-Aid Acid Test, by Tom Wolfe, explores the life of Ken Kesey following the publication of *One Flew Over the Cuckoo's Nest* and *Sometimes a Great Notion.* Wolfe documents the rampant drug use of the Merry Pranksters and recounts Kesey's run-ins with local and federal law enforcement agencies, his exile to Mexico, his imprisonment, and his status as a progenitor of the 1960s counterculture. Farrar, Straus and Giroux, Inc., 1968.

It's easy to find books published by Wiley Publishing, Inc. or these other publishers. You'll find them in your favorite bookstores (on the Internet and at a store near you). We also have three Web sites that you can use to read about all the books we publish:

- www.cliffsnotes.com
- www.dummies.com
- www.wiley.com

Magazines and Journals

Magazines and journals are excellent for additional information about *One Flew Over the Cuckoo's Nest* by Ken Kesey. You may want to check out these publications for information about the author and/or related works:

BOYERS, ROBERT. "Attitudes toward Sex in American 'High Culture'," *The Annals of the American Academy of Political and Social Science,* Vol. 376, March 1968, pp. 36-52. While admiring Kesey's restraint in portraying the hospital as symbolic of civilization as a whole, Boyers finds Kesey's depiction of sex as the ultimate expression of human freedom as too simplistic. Boyers also finds that the ends McMurphy desires don't always justify the means he employs to accomplish them.

MALIN, IRVING. "Ken Kesey: *One Flew Over the Cuckoo's Nest,* Critique: Studies in Modern Fiction, Vol. V, No. 2, Fall 1962, pp. 81-84. Malin asserts that the novel should be read more as a poem than as a philosophical treatise on freedom from oppression. He admires Kesey's use of imagery, which he believes adequately conveys the book's meaning.

SASSOON, R. L. *Northwest Review,* Vol. 6, No. 2, Spring 1963, pp. 116-120. Sassoon perceives Kesey's novel as an admonishment to modern humanity for its inability to listen to itself in order to overcome external oppression. Sassoon also comments on the mythical properties of the novel, which the critic believes redeems a perceived superficial indictment of society as a whole.

SHERWOOD, TERRY G. "*One Flew Over the Cuckoo's Nest* and the Comic Strip," *Critique: Studies in Modern Fiction*, Vol. 13, No. 1, 1970, pp. 96-109. Sherwood argues that Kesey's use of comic book and other popular culture motifs indicate a serious artistic manifesto that have been overshadowed by Kesey's counterculture reputation. Sherwood also identifies and explicates the folk songs sung by McMurphy, while finding that Kesey's indictment of society's morality is oversimplified and sentimentalized.

SUTHERLAND, JANET R. "A Defense of Ken Kesey's *One Flew Over the Cuckoo's Nest*," *English Journal*, Vol. 61, No. 1, January 1972, pp. 28-31. Sutherland defends the novel against censorship in high school literature courses. Sutherland considers the obscenity and immorality of the book to be confined to the actions perpetrated by Nurse Ratched and the hospital staff against McMurphy and the patients, and concludes that students should be allowed to read the book as a matter of freedom of speech.

Internet

Check out these Web resources for more information about Ken Kesey and *One Flew Over the Cuckoo's Nest*:

Ken Kesey, http://www.charm.net/~brooklyn/People/KenKesey.html—Presents a biography of Kesey and links to sites with bibliographies and memorabilia on the author.

One Flew over the Cuckoo's Nest—Memorable Moments, http://www.filmsite.org/onef.html—includes a synopsis of the film and extensive quotes from the screenplay.

One Flew Over the Cuckoo's Nest, http://members.tripod.com/~mvault/cuckoonest.htm—features a film synopsis and facts about the film's cast and Ken Kesey.

One Flew Over the Cuckoo's Nest: The Missing Parts, http://www.redhousebooks.com/galleries/cuckoo.htm—presents original versions of sections of the novel that Kesey was forced to rewrite due to the threat of a libel suit by a nurse Kesey worked with.

Vocabulary from One Flew Over the Cuckoo's Nest, http://www.vocabulary.com/Vuctcuckoo.html—features a list of words in each section of the novel that might prove difficult for high school readers.

Next time you're on the Internet, don't forget to drop by www.cliffsnotes.com. We created an online Resource Center that you can use today, tomorrow, and beyond.

Films and Other Recordings

The following films either explain or adapt *One Flew Over the Cuckoo's Next* or contain themes that reflect the novel's antiauthoritarian message:

Fight Club—The first half of the 1999 film starring Brad Pitt, Edward Norton, and Helena Bonham Carter comically presents a dehumanized world that has emasculated and feminized men.

Great Books Library, Discover Channel School, http://www.discoveryschool.com—Narrated by Donald Sutherland, this thirty-minute documentary presents dramatizations of key scenes from the perspective of Chief Bromden, includes filmed interviews with Kesey, and extensive footage of the Merry Pranksters and the Further bus tour.

One Flew Over the Cuckoo's Nest—The 1975 film, considered a cinematic classic, features Jack Nicholson and Louise Fletcher in Academy Award winning performances as, respectively, Randle Patrick McMurphy and Nurse Ratched. The film also won Academy Awards for Best Picture and Best Director, the latter won by Milos Forman.

Pink Floyd's The Wall—This 1980s adaptation of the classic song cycle by the band Pink Floyd presents many images by the artist Gerald Scarfe that capture the many ways society can enslave the individual. The song "Mother" could easily serve as Billy Bibbit's theme.

Send Us Your Favorite Tips

In your quest for knowledge, have you ever experienced that sublime moment when you figure out a trick that saves time or trouble? Perhaps you realized you were taking ten steps to accomplish something that could have taken two. Or you found a little-known workaround that achieved great results. If you've discovered a useful tip that helped you retain information more effectively and you'd like to share it, the

CliffsNotes staff would love to hear from you. Go to our Web site at www.cliffsnotes.com and click the Talk to Us button. If we select your tip, we may publish it as part of CliffsNotes Daily, our exciting, free e-mail newsletter. To find out more or to subscribe to a newsletter, go to www.cliffsnotes.com on the Web.

Index

P

paranoia, Chief's, 6, 17, 75, 80
patients. *See* Acutes; Chronics; characters
   listed by name
Pink Floyd's The Wall, 95
Pitt, Brad, 87
plot synopsis, 6–9
Public Relations man, 24, 29, 74

R

Ratched, Nurse
   described, 6, 9
   doctors, 24, 27, 90
   exposed as human, 8, 68
   inflates self, 16–17
   log book spying among patients, 22
   McMurphy's assessment, 7, 51
   name, nature, 73
   plans to keep McMurphy, 41
   quotation, 90
   threatens patients, 47
   turns patients against each other, 7, 21,
      27, 78
   turns patients against McMurphy, 61–63
Rawler, Old, 11
rebellion, McMurphy's
   attacks Ratched, 68
   fishing trip, 55
   music, request to turn down, 32
   nurses; station, retrieves cigarettes, 53
   shower fight, 62
   television votes, 35, 39
   towel scene, 30
rebels, other films
   Cool Hand Luke, 87
   Fight Club, 87–88, 95
   Mr. Roberts, 86
   Shawshank Redemption, The, 87
Redfield, William, 80
religious imagery
   apostles, 59, 84, 85
   betrayal, 68, 85
   Cool Hand Luke, 87
   crown of thorns, 6
   crucifixion, 6, 84, 85
   Last Supper, 73, 85
   redemption through laughter, 83–84
resident doctors, 24
Robbins, Tim, 87
Ruckly, 11, 22

S

Sailor Song, 3
Sampson, Will, 80
Sandy. *See* Gilfilliam, Sandy
Santa Claus patient, 28
Sassoon, R. L, 93
Scanlon, 10, 55
Sea Lion, The, 3
Sefelt, 10, 47
Shawshank Redemption, The, 87
Sherwood, Terry G., 94
size metaphor
   Chief's father shrinks, 79
   Chief's mother, 75
   Chief's self-image, 16, 19, 56
   McMurphy seems large, 19
   patients grow, 46
   Ratched inflates self, 16–17, 19
Small, Marya, 80
Sometimes a Great Notion, 3
Spivey, Doctor
   Acutes meeting, 26
   described, 11
   joins fishing trip, 58
   Ratched controls, 27, 90
   stands up to Ratched, 32, 55
Stanford University, 2
Starr, Candy, 12, 58, 66
suffocation, 6, 8, 68, 85
suicide
   Bibbit's, 68, 85
   Bibbit's previous attempt, 76, 90
   castration, 38
   Cheswick's, 7, 46, 73, 81–82, 89
Sutherland, Janet R., 94
synopsis, plot, 6–9

T

Taber, Max, 10, 24
Tadem, 11
tattoo, McMurphy's, 57
temperature imagery, 42
therapy sessions
   McMurphy enters, 26
   patients take over, 45, 46
   Ratched controls, 21, 27, 78
   Ratched punishes group for rebellion, 53
   Ratched suggests lobotomy, 66
   television vote, 39
Turkle, Mr., 12, 29

NOTES

NOTES